REAL VALOR

Boaz men

* **Believe** and act on Gods Word
P. 12

* Don't **Bolt** - pp. 33-47

* **Built** on the Rock Not Sand.

* House of **Bread** - white or Wheat
P. 15

* Works hard to avoid making
Bad Decisions

* are **big** on Reliability, dependability
and Faithfulness.

* Are the **best** example of
Christ to his family and world.

REAL VALOR

A CHARGE TO NURTURE AND PROTECT YOUR FAMILY

STEVE FARRAR

David C Cook®

transforming lives together

REAL VALOR
Published by David C Cook
4050 Lee Vance View
Colorado Springs, CO 80918 U.S.A.

David C Cook Distribution Canada
55 Woodslee Avenue, Paris, Ontario, Canada N3L 3E5

David C Cook U.K., Kingsway Communications
Eastbourne, East Sussex BN23 6NT, England

The graphic circle C logo is a registered trademark of David C Cook.

The website addresses recommended throughout this book are offered as a
resource to you. These websites are not intended in any way to be or imply an
endorsement on the part of David C Cook, nor do we vouch for their content.

Unless otherwise noted, all Scripture quotations are taken from The Holy Bible, English
Standard Version® (ESV®), copyright © 2001 by Crossway, a publishing ministry of Good
News Publishers. Used by permission. All rights reserved. Scripture quotations marked KJV
are taken from the King James Version of the Bible. (Public Domain); NASB are taken from the
New American Standard Bible®, Copyright © 1960, 1995 by The Lockman Foundation. Used
by permission. (www.Lockman.org); NIV are taken from the Holy Bible, New International
Version®, NIV®. Copyright © 1973, 1984 by Biblica, Inc.™ Used by permission of Zondervan.
All rights reserved worldwide. www.zondervan.com; and NLT are taken from the *Holy Bible,
New Living Translation*, copyright © 1996, 2007 by Tyndale House Foundation. Used by
permission of Tyndale House Publishers, Inc., Carol Stream, Illinois 60188. All rights reserved.
The author has added italics to Scripture quotations for emphasis.

LCCN 2013930788
ISBN 978-1-4347-6867-4
eISBN 978-1-4347-0557-0

© 2013 Steve Farrar
Published in association with the literary agency of WordServe Literary
Group, Ltd., 10152 S. Knoll Circle, Highlands Ranch, CO 80130.

The Team: Don Pape, Larry Libby, Amy Konyndyk, Karen Lee-
Thorp, Jack Campbell, Renada Arens, Karen Athen
Cover Design: Nick Lee

Printed in the United States of America
First Edition 2013

1 2 3 4 5 6 7 8 9 10

012813

To Court and Rachel
The modern version of an old story

CONTENTS

ACKNOWLEDGMENTS

Thanks to three men who were instrumental in getting this work into your hands.

- Don Pape—who oversees the publishing team at David C Cook.
- Larry Libby—my longtime editor and friend.
- Greg Johnson—who hunts and scouts on my behalf in the publishing world.

It just wouldn't happen without them, and for their efforts I am grateful.

And thanks to one great woman—my wife, Mary—who for thirty-five years has been more to me than I could ever express here. I don't believe in luck—but I do believe in God's providence, and I "providenced" out when she came into my life.

CHAPTER ONE

BOAZ MAN

"The wind in a man's face makes him wise."
—John Ray

Right out of the chute, this is a book that centers on Boaz, but I want to begin this book about Boaz by quoting a Scripture concerning his great-grandson.

> He chose David his servant
> and took him from the sheepfolds;
> from following the nursing ewes he brought him
> to shepherd Jacob his people,
> Israel his inheritance.

With upright heart he shepherded them

and guided them with his skillful hand. (Ps. 78:70–72)

David, as you know, was one of the great kings of Israel. Yes, he'd had his share of significant and even shocking sin. But David was a man after God's own heart, and even when he fell into deep sin, he demonstrated deep repentance.

In other words, when he went wrong, he went *way* wrong. But when he turned around and came back to God, he came back heart and soul.

Overall, he was a king with a track record of following the Lord with a whole heart. Note the words set down in his Old Testament obituary: *With upright heart he shepherded them and guided them with his skillful hand.*

David started out as a shepherd and remained a shepherd his entire life. From the earliest days of his youth, he guided and cared for the little lambs and later was promoted to be king over God's people. In Israel, God expected His kings to shepherd the nation and its people. And David pulled it off with a skillful hand.

Joel Beeke told the story of an old Welsh shepherd who was asked how long it took for a shepherd to become competent. The old sheepherder paused for a moment and then replied, "About four generations."[1]

David was a remarkable shepherd. But David's shepherding skills didn't start with him. It started with his great-grandfather Boaz. Oh, and by the way, if you do the math, David is the fourth generation from Boaz.

David shepherded a nation.

Boaz shepherded two desperate and destitute women, saving their lives. Eventually, he married the younger woman, took in her needy mother-in-law, and raised a son. In other words, he shepherded his family.

Most men don't shepherd nations. God calls most men to be husbands and fathers and grandfathers. *He calls them to shepherd their families.* We don't fly around in *Air Force One* and ride in limos. We aren't kings—we're family men. But as someone once said, "Every family is a small civilization."

I'm to shepherd my family as I follow the Lord Jesus Christ. But first He must do a radical work in my heart to turn me from myself and my sin to know and follow Him.

Owen Strachan said it well:

> This very day, every man—whether a global leader or an unknown tradesman—has an opportunity to show the world that the gospel does not kill pleasure or aggressiveness. Rather, as [Jonathan] Edwards has shown, it frees Christians to experience true pleasure and to act in manly ways for a far greater cause than ourselves. We grieve the trajectory of modern men, and we feel special pain for the wives and children who are, through no fault of their own, deeply damaged by the sins of men. In a broken world, we pray to God to show the world a better way, a greater joy, and a magnificent Savior, who delights in taking sinful men and turning them into agents of his glory.[2]

That's what it means to be a Boaz Man.

I will never have what it takes to do the job in my home until I utter from my heart of hearts, *"The Lord is my Shepherd."*

Boaz did that, and he did it well. He was one of the few who trusted in the Lord in a time of tremendous wickedness. His nation was in freefall and decline. And all the while, he stood firm like a pillar of basalt, going about his business, shunning sin on the left and the right, and trusting the Great Shepherd to direct his steps and provide wisdom for the daily grind.

Sometimes you hear people in Christian circles talk about miracles, signs, and wonders. As far as I'm concerned, a man who stays faithful to God and shepherds his family in a time of national upheaval and great moral decline is a wonder. And something about him points to strength and wisdom beyond his own.

Boaz is among the group of Old Testament greats who point us to Christ. I think you're going to like this guy.

He reminds us by his life and character of what it means to be a God-fearing man. We live in a time when so many are confused about masculinity and manhood. They never really saw their fathers model manly, godly behavior in the home. As a result, they're confused and unsure of what they're supposed to do and how they're supposed to live. Some of them get so overwhelmed that they just give up.

"I Don't Need to Be Confused"

Jackie Cooper was a big-time TV star when I was growing up. He had a couple of major hits in primetime, including *Hennessy*. When Jackie Cooper was a kid, he was one of Hollywood's biggest child movie stars—sort of the male equivalent to Shirley Temple. Then he performed on the stage in London and on Broadway. After he left his primetime TV gig, he became a Hollywood producer and director. For a while he tried his hand at car racing. Later he raised thoroughbred horses.

So here's a guy who was successful in many different facets of show business his entire life. He was talented, smart, funny, and very engaging. And he was also a pretty good businessman. That's why I took a moment to read his obituary when I saw it online.

And I found out something I didn't know about him.

Jackie Cooper had never known his father. His dad cut out on the family in 1924 when Jackie was just two years old. In 1951, Cooper was driving his car from New York to Los Angeles. Apparently, at that point in his life he didn't like flying and chose to make the cross-country trip in his car. He pulled into a service station one afternoon in some small town outside of Kansas City to get some gas and a Coke. As he was pumping gas, the mechanic recognized him and came over to greet him. Jackie Cooper shook the man's hand and was stunned to hear the man tell him that his father, John Cooper Sr., lived upstairs over the garage.

Cooper had to be in shock. The man went on to say that his father had Jackie's pictures all over his room and spoke of him with pride. "Let me tell him that you're here," the mechanic said.

"Please don't," replied Cooper. "I don't need to be confused."

And then Jackie Cooper got into his car and drove away.[3]

You see, that's what happens when a man runs away and doesn't shepherd his family. When a man doesn't care enough to stay on the scene and love and care for his family, all he leaves behind him is a cloud of confusion.

White or Wheat?

We need to take a minute and talk about white bread and whole grain bread. That may seem to you like a jarring shift of gears, but I assure you, it isn't. I think there are two kinds of men in the world: you've got your white bread men and your whole grain men.

Jackie Cooper's father was a white bread man.

Maybe your dad was too.

Allow me to explain. For thousands of years, bread has been the staple of life. Much care and time has been given to the planting, nurturing, and harvesting of the various kinds of grains. For generations upon generations, virtually all bread produced was whole grain bread. But somewhere around a hundred years ago, somebody (and it's hard to determine who) got the bright idea of removing the bran and the germ from whole wheat flour. And when they did that, they basically stripped it of its nutritional value.

But the new milling process also had a benefit. It greatly increased the shelf life of the bread before it went stale.

The white of white bread, however, wasn't that easy to come by. It seems that when you mill out the wheat germ and bran from the bread, it leaves it with an unappetizing yellowish color. That's when they got the idea of bleaching the flour with chlorine dioxide gas, to make it white.

This stuff was easy to mass-produce, slice, and package. It was snow white, uniform, perfectly sliced—and essentially worthless, nutritionally speaking. It looked like bread, but in essence it had no substance. So eventually they had to start adding minerals to it to keep the soldiers healthy in World War II.

(I'm going somewhere with this, so stay with me.)

The good stuff in the bread world is whole grain bread. Did you know that there is actually a recipe for bread that God gave for the Israelites to eat? We've got some Ezekiel 4:9 bread in our freezer. No kidding—that's the name of the bread. The bread recipe is actually based on Ezekiel 4:9, and the passage is paraphrased on the packaging: "Take also unto thee wheat and barley, and beans, and lentils, and millet, and spelt, and put them in one vessel, and make bread of it."

This company actually did that—and they made a remarkable discovery. And once again I quote from the label on the plastic bag: "We discovered that when these six grains and legumes are sprouted and combined, an amazing thing happens. A complete protein is created that closely parallels the protein found in milk and eggs. In fact, the protein quality is so high … that it contains all 9 essential amino acids. There are 18 amino acids present in this unique bread—from all vegetable sources—naturally balanced in nature."

Now that's what I call wonder bread. It's got all the substance and all the stuff that you need to stay healthy.

Okay—you get the point.

White bread men are men who look just like real men, but they don't have the substance needed to nurture and provide for their families. These guys look good on the surface, but they don't deliver in the clutch. They're like a mouthful of … nothing.

That's the kind of father Jackie Cooper had.

But the Boaz Man is the whole grain man. Yes, he's probably kind of rough around the edges. He may be a little lumpy and bumpy, his coloring isn't always perfect, his texture may be a little more coarse, and sometimes you've got to chew a little longer to digest what he has to say. But he's got the substance and stuff to stay the course and take care of his family in the stresses and strains of everyday life.

The Book of Boaz

So let's get to the book of Boaz.

But there's just one problem. The book of Boaz doesn't exist.

The book of Ruth, however, *does* exist, and it is in that brief Old Testament book that we find the story of Boaz. So who was Ruth? She was the woman who wound up marrying Boaz, a distant relative of her mother-in-law, Naomi.

Wait a minute. If Ruth already had a mother-in-law, then that means she was already married. Right? That's true—but her husband died as a young man, and Ruth became a very young widow. As a matter of fact, both Ruth and Naomi were widows—and they were in a heap of trouble.

Until Boaz showed up.

And then Ruth met Boaz and everything changed for the better.

This may be hard for you to believe, but your life has actually been improved beyond words because Boaz walked into Ruth's life. (But I'm getting way ahead of myself here.)

There is no book of Boaz, but there is the book of Ruth.

Nevertheless, even though he doesn't get top billing, Boaz is the central figure in the story. As a matter of fact, if Boaz had never showed up, there would be no story.

The book of Ruth has only four chapters and three main people: Naomi, Ruth, and Boaz. But every time I read through the book of Ruth, I come away with the same thought.

The book of Ruth is all about Boaz.

He doesn't even show up until chapter 2, but when he does, he rescues two women who are in desperate financial straits with absolutely no options to improve their lives. And then Boaz shows up and saves their lives.

Matthew Henry, the great Bible commentator of the nineteenth century, said that the book of Boaz—the book of Ruth—had two purposes. The first was to lead us to the doctrine of God's providence, and the second was to lead us to Christ.[4]

If you've ever doubted that God is involved in every detail of your life, you will be reminded of that fact on every page of the book of Boaz. Your life is not an accident or a mistake or the result of chance. You are alive and exist by the specific plan and will of God. That's true of you and it's true of the history of the entire world. Every detail of the past and of the future are planned, arranged, and orchestrated by the providence of God.

Did you know that it's impossible to be content where you are right now without an awareness of God's providence? The reason that so many of us struggle with contentment is because we are woefully ignorant of what the Bible teaches us about God's providence. The book of Boaz is all about God's providence, and it's all about the Lord Jesus Christ—and it's providence that ties the two together.

Over three hundred years ago, Jeremiah Burroughs wrote about the contentment that only a right understanding of God's providence can bring. These are whole-grain words. Chew them slowly, and take in all their nourishment.

> (It is necessary) to understand the universality of providence, that it, how the providence of God goes through the whole world and extends itself to everything. Not only that God by his providence rules the world, and governs all things in general, but that it reaches to every detail; not

only to order the great affairs of kingdoms, but it reaches to every man's family; it reaches to every person in the family; it reaches to every condition; yes, to every happening, to everything that falls out concerning you in every particular; not one hair falls from your head, not a sparrow to the ground, without the providence of God. Nothing befalls you, good or evil, but there is a providence of the eternal first Being in that thing; and therein is God's infiniteness, that it reaches to the least things, to the worm that is under your feet.[5]

Not only does God take care of the whole world, but His care extends to the very worms in the earth beneath your feet. When Jeremiah Burroughs penned that truth in the 1600s, he wasn't sipping a Snapple Diet Peach Tea. But the other day when I took the cap off a Snapple bottle, I read an interesting fact inside the bottle cap. Worms (so the bottle cap told me) have five hearts that are perfectly synchronized. That was news to me—especially since I had just looked at the Jeremiah Burroughs comment about the God's providence extending even to worms.

So I did a computer search on this and found that technically worms don't have hearts but five aortic arches that for simplicity's sake are commonly called "hearts." The aortic arch functions as a heart, although there are no chambers. "Worms also don't have lungs. They absorb oxygen through their skin and then it gets into their blood vessels. The dorsal blood vessel does a bit of the pumping work, with the hearts helping to keep the blood pressure steady."[6]

I know you have a pretty busy life with a lot going on, but take a minute to think about how God regulates blood pressure. Not your blood pressure, but the blood pressure of the earthworms in the ground below you. That's how detailed the providence of God truly is. He governs the entire universe, and if He even governs the blood pressure of worms, that simple fact should reduce *your* blood pressure. In other words, if He's taking care of the worms, He's obviously got you covered too.

Naomi and Ruth didn't know much about worms, but they did understand that their credit cards were maxed out, the cupboards were pretty much bare, and they were out of cash. Boaz showed up in just the nick of time for these destitute women. They were without government assistance, savings accounts, or food stamps.

Then … at the exact moment when they were about to lose hope, Boaz saw Ruth. And in that one detail that fed through the optic nerve of the physiology of Boaz, both of their lives changed in an instant. I would even be so bold as to say that the whole world changed in that moment. And it was all because of the providence of God.

Maybe you've heard that old expression "The devil is in the details." No, the fact is *God* is in the details. And one small detail, like Boaz seeing Ruth from afar for the first time, contains not one providence but many providences. Jeremiah Burroughs continued:

> There is an infinite variety of the works of God in an ordinary providence, and yet they all work in an orderly way. We put these two things together, for God in his providence causes a thousand thousand things to depend upon one another. There are an infinite number of wheels, as I may say, in the works of providence; put together all the works that ever God did from all eternity or ever will do, and they all make up but one work, and they have been as several wheels that have had their ordinary motion to attain the end that God from all eternity has appointed.
>
> We, indeed, look at things by pieces, we look at one detail and do not consider the relation that one thing has to another, but God looks at all things at once, and sees the relation that one thing has to another. When a child looks

at a clock, it looks first at one wheel, and then at another wheel; he does not look at them together or the dependence that one has on another; but the workman has his eyes on them all together and sees the dependence of all, one upon another; so it is God's providence. Now notice how this works to contentment; when a certain passage of providence befalls me, that is one wheel, and it may be that if this wheel were stopped, a thousand other things might come to be stopped by this. In a clock, stop but one wheel and you stop every wheel because they are dependent upon one another. So when God has ordered a thing for the present to be thus and thus, how do you know how many things depend on this thing? God may have some work to do twenty years hence that depends on this passage of providence that falls out this day or this week.[7]

The fact that Boaz saw Ruth was more than a single man noticing a lovely woman from a distance. It was more than your average boy-meets-girl account.

Generations were impacted by that moment.

Without that moment, there would have been no King David born in Bethlehem four generations in the future. And what then of that other King born in Bethlehem—the One who would be known as King of Kings and Lord of Lords? All of this was providentially connected to Boaz and Ruth.

Matthew Henry was right: the book of Ruth leads us to Christ. There are two genealogies of the Lord Jesus recorded in the New Testament. They can be found in Matthew 1:1–17 and Luke 3:23–38. Boaz is found in both genealogies, and his wife, Ruth, is included in the Matthew account.

In both instances, Joseph is mentioned as the husband of Mary but not as the father of Jesus. Jesus was born of a virgin. But the man Joseph, to whom she was betrothed (engaged in our terms), was a direct descendant of Boaz.

Here's the providence of God: if Boaz had not married Ruth, they would obviously have no descendants. And that would simply mean that hundreds of years later, Joseph would not have been betrothed to Mary, the young virgin who would be the mother of the Lord Jesus.

Sinclair Ferguson homes in on the theme of the book of Boaz:

> This is where the book of Ruth comes in. It focuses like a microscope on part of the detailed preparation God made to fulfill his purposes in redemptive history. Apparently the story of a small and insignificant family, it is actually one of the building blocks in God's preparatory work as He sovereignly directed history towards the coming of the Savior Jesus Christ. In fact, the message of the book of Ruth cannot be fully understood apart from the coming of our Lord Jesus Christ. In that sense, studying it will help us to understand Christ himself—and, indeed, the whole Bible—more fully and clearly.[8]

Boaz ... and You

So what does Boaz have to do with you and your daily life and pressures? Consider this: *it means that God has a detailed and providential plan that He is working in your life—even when it seems like your life is dull and boring.*

Troy Meeder, in his excellent book, *Average Joe*, described our struggle as we seemingly just plod through everyday life:

> As a boy I certainly had bigger plans than working in a cramped cubicle from eight to five, building widgets on the late shift at the local mill, or flipping burgers at the corner

diner. My boyhood dreams never included a mortgage, diapers, traffic tickets, or cleaning out the gutters. Perhaps, like me, you dreamed of saving a life, flying a fighter jet, finding a cure for cancer, or even walking on the moon.

As boys, we had such high hopes to accomplish something great, to make a difference, to live a life that left a mark on those around us. We marveled at men like Chuck Yeager, Neil Armstrong, Buzz Aldrin, and the Reverend Billy Graham. We wanted to ride like John Wayne, lead like Ronald Reagan, drive like Mario Andretti, and win like the 1973 Miami Dolphins.

Maybe you are asking the same question I ask: *What happened to my life?*

What happened for most of us is *reality*. Instead of finding fame and fortune, normalcy and "never enough" found us. We are average Joes, but is that really a problem? Definitely not! So-called average Joes are the ones who make the world work.

God seems to have a special fondness for average Joes. Before they accomplished extraordinary deeds, normal guys like Gideon, David, Peter, and Paul went about their farming, sheep herding, fishing, and tent making. Even Jesus, our Redeemer, Healer, and coming King, started out using a hammer and saw in a carpenter's shop.

You'll find average Joes are everywhere. Good men, honest men. They are hard working, genuine, and steadfast.[9]

That's why we need to take a long, hard look at Boaz. He was a godly man and a good man. He was hardworking, genuine, and steadfast. In other words, he was an average Joe just going about his daily life. There was nothing all that exciting or earthshaking in his daily routines—but God was at work in every detail and circumstance of his life, weaving it all together for good. And that good was not only for him, but also for generations of his children yet to come.

By the way, that's exactly what the Lord is doing in your life. Seriously—that's exactly what He is doing. But we rarely think about that because we're so worn out from just trying to cover all of the bases. I'm sure Boaz had many days when he felt the same way.

I can hear some guy somewhere saying, "Wait a minute—hold it right there! You're wrong about Boaz—he wasn't an average Joe like Troy Meeder was describing." If you're the guy who's thinking that, you're familiar with chapter 2, verse 1 of the book of Boaz (Ruth). In the King James Version, Boaz is described as "a mighty man of wealth."

A mighty man of wealth is no average Joe.

But let's take a closer look at this word. The English Standard Version renders it "a worthy man." In fact, the notes in the ESV Study Bible are helpful here: *Worthy* (in Hebrew *hayil*, literally, "of worth or excellence") connotes character, wealth, position, or strength.

Boaz probably had a few bucks put away because he was a sensible man and a hard worker, but the emphasis is on the excellence and worth of his character. In other words, his influence and the strength of his position in the community came primarily out of his character not his bank account. Dr. Leon Morris, a noted Old Testament scholar, put this all in very clear English for us:

> The exact expression rendered a mighty man of wealth (AV, RV) is elsewhere translated "a mighty man of valour" (e.g., Judges 11:1). We perhaps get the force of it by thinking of our word "knight". This applied originally to a man distinguished for military prowess, but is now used widely of those whose excellence lies in other fields. In the Old Testament it most often has to do with fighting capacity.

Boaz may have been a warrior, for these were troubled times and any man might have to fight. But in this book he appears rather as a solid citizen, a man of influence and integrity in the community and it is likely that this is what the term denotes here.[10]

Boaz, the whole-grain man, modeled the truths of Philippians 2:3–4 (NASB):

> Do nothing from selfishness or empty conceit, but with humility of mind regard one another as more important than yourselves; do not merely look out for your own personal interests, but also for the interests of others.

I imagine that Jackie Cooper's father had all kinds of excuses for walking out and disappearing from his son's life. But when push comes to shove, he was selfish and looked out for his own interests. He was neither a good citizen nor a good father. That's how you confuse a boy, and that's how you destroy a family, a community, and a nation.

John Flavel made a penetrating observation over three hundred years ago, and it applies to our day:

> Upon their king's death, it was the Persians' custom (I am not saying it was laudable) to grant everyone liberty for five days to do whatever they wanted. The unbridled lust was so great that it made the people long and pray for the installment of the next king.[11]

When everyone has unchecked liberty, all hell breaks loose. It's called *anarchy*, and it is demonic. And there is nothing like unchecked liberty to make people long for a good king and good laws.

There was nothing wrong with Jackie Cooper's father except one thing: he had the wrong king in his life. When you are the king of your own life, you give yourself permission to do anything you want—and that's when all hell breaks loose. In the process, a lot of vulnerable people around you get bruised, crushed, and broken by your "freedom."

Not to mention confused.

The only way to fix that is to get a new King in your life. The Lord Jesus Christ is the Lord of Lords and King of Kings.

In that same Phillipians 2 passage, the Lord Jesus was immediately offered as the solution to human selfishness, sin, and personal anarchy:

> Do nothing from selfishness or empty conceit, but with humility of mind regard one another as more important than yourselves; do not merely look out for your own personal interests, but also for the interests of others. Have this attitude in yourselves which was also in Christ Jesus, who, although He existed in the form of God, did not regard equality with God a thing to be grasped, but emptied Himself, taking the form of a bond-servant, and being made in the likeness of men. Being found in appearance as a man, He humbled Himself by becoming obedient to the point of death, even death on a cross. For this reason also, God highly exalted Him, and bestowed on Him the name which is above every name, so that at the name of Jesus every knee will bow, of those who are in heaven and on earth and under the earth, and that every tongue will confess that Jesus Christ is Lord, to the glory of God the Father. (vv. 3–11 NASB)

The Lord Jesus is our soon-coming King and the ultimate picture of what it means to be a Boaz Man. As we will see in a later chapter, Boaz acted as a kinsman-redeemer in saving Ruth. It's one of the best and most beautiful pictures in all of Scripture of what the Lord Jesus has done for us.

He saves us from sin, He saves us from ourselves, He saves us from selfishness, and He enables us by His grace to serve and to look out for the interests of others. That's the kind of man you are called to be. And only the Lord Jesus, the ultimate Boaz, can turn you into that kind of man.

Any other solution is just white bread.

**A Boaz Man follows the Great Shepherd
and shepherds his family.**

CHAPTER TWO

WHITE BREAD GONE BAD

"A man may have the tongue of an angel, and the heart of a devil."
—John Flavel

Bankers are taking a public relations hit these days. Of course, bankers are like anyone else—some are good and some are bad. That's also true of preachers, plumbers, and politicians.

The Boaz Man, as we saw in the last chapter, is a solid citizen and family man, a man of character and integrity who operates out of servanthood, rather than selfishness or greed. Because the Lord Jesus Christ is King of his life, he in turn serves his King by serving others. That's the Boaz Man in nutshell. Christ has changed his heart and therefore changed his behavior.

A Boaz Man in the Clutch

Where were you in 1906? Unless you're the world's oldest man, you probably weren't around. Shortly after 5:00 a.m., April 18, 1906, a killer earthquake hit the San Francisco Bay Area. Thousands were rousted out of bed by the shaking and swaying of their homes and apartments, including one banker who was asleep in his home in San Mateo, a suburb seventeen miles south of the city. It took him nearly six hours to get to his office in the city to see what was left of his bank building.

[A. P. Giannini] was the owner of the Bank of Italy (the precursor to today's Bank of America), and he knew he had to see what had happened to his building. What he soon discovered was that it wasn't the quake itself that caused most of the destruction. Fires came later from so many wood stoves tipping over during the temblor and the burst gas pipes. That's what really decimated San Francisco. Giannini took a horse and wagon filled with vegetables to the city and soon discovered that his worst fears had been realized. The building was in shambles. But after searching through what remained, he eventually found the vault containing $2 million in gold, coins, and securities. That's where the horse and wagon came in handy.

With flames getting closer by the minute, Giannini filled the wagon with the money and covered them all with vegetables so no one could see what he had. His horses pulled what must have been an incredibly heavy load down to the waterfront. There he set up a workspace of sorts, by placing boards across two barrels. Between that impromptu office and his wagon load of money, he was the only banker in San Francisco to stay open for business. Customers were

30

able to come to him and borrow the money they needed to restart their lives. Every other bank in the city kept their doors shut until much later.[1]

Giannini built his bank by loaning to the working men who couldn't get loans from other banks. He would assess his loans on the basis of a man's character, not his financial position or his family connections. It was Giannini who gave hardworking immigrants from all over the world a chance to make it.

And he wasn't going to let an earthquake stop him.

When the city was devastated by earthquake and fire, he would tell everyone who came to his makeshift counter on the pier that together they would rebuild their town.

That's what you call a Boaz move when so many others were in panic. Giannini wasn't looking for a government bailout; he just started bailing— lending money to men who were willing work and rebuild.

Giannini lent to the little guy when the little guy needed it most. In return, the little guy made deposits at Giannini's bank. As San Francisco moved from chaos to order, from order to growth, from growth to prosperity, Giannini lent more to the little guy, and the little guy banked even more with Giannini. The bank gained momentum, little guy by little guy, loan by loan, deposit by deposit, branch by branch, across California, renaming itself Bank of America along the way. In October 1945, it became the largest commercial bank in the world.[2]

A. P. Giannini was the best citizen in San Francisco when the earthquake hit. He didn't bolt from the city—he went *into* the city. And by his actions, he made it possible for others to start rebuilding their lives in the midst of great disaster.

That's a Boaz kind of man. That's a Boaz kind of move.

In my reading of Giannini's life, I don't see that he ever personally embraced the gospel of Christ. I certainly hope that he did and that I will meet him someday on the other side. What can't be argued, however, was that this man personally governed his life by biblical principles. It came out in the way he ran his business and in his devotion to his wife, children, and community.

Giannini had what you might call a biblical worldview. Kip Fry commented:

> When all was said and done, A. P. Giannini had rescued several different movie studios during the early days of the industry, revitalized the state's wine business, financed construction of the Golden Gate Bridge in San Francisco, created the notion of branch banking, and even had an iconic film character styled after him (George Bailey in the Frank Capra classic "It's a Wonderful Life").[3]

When a man has a biblical worldview, he lives differently from other men—especially in the clutch.

In fact, that's the very place where a Boaz Man really shines.

A Weak Man with a Strong Name

The book of Boaz is about three key people: Naomi, Ruth, and Boaz. But the story doesn't begin with Boaz—nor Ruth for that matter. Both of these come in later. The book begins with a man named Elimelech.

And Elimelech was the anti-Boaz.

Let's just say up front that Elimelech probably couldn't have obtained a loan from A. P. Giannini. He was just a little too slick. He was one of those guys who was always looking more for an angle than he was for hard work.

Elimelech isn't what you'd call a key player in the story. The fact is, he gets a very brief mention, and much of what we surmise about him has to be read between the lines.

Does that mean he was unimportant? No, in a sense he was actually pivotal to the entire providential story the Lord was unfolding through Boaz.

God is providential over the good and bad in all of life.

Boaz was the good guy and wore the white hat. Elimelech was the bad guy and wore the black hat. And the result of Elimelech's poor decisions was the devastation of his family.

> In the days when the judges ruled there was a famine in the land, and a man of Bethlehem in Judah went to sojourn in the country of Moab, he and his wife and his two sons. The name of the man was Elimelech and the name of his wife Naomi, and the names of his two sons were Mahlon and Chilion. They were Ephrathites from Bethlehem in Judah. They went into the country of Moab and remained there. But Elimelech, the husband of Naomi, died, and she was left with her two sons. These took Moabite wives; the name of the one was Orpah and the name of the other Ruth. They lived there about ten years, and both Mahlon and Chilion died, so that the woman was left without her two sons and her husband. (Ruth 1:1–5)

Elimelech Lived in a Bad Time

How do we know that he lived in a bad period of history? The text tells us right out of the blocks that the story occurs "in the days when the judges ruled."

The previous book before the book of Boaz is Judges. Judges covers approximately three hundred years of Israel's history. It basically begins with the death of Joshua, who had made this statement at the end of his life:

> Now therefore fear the LORD and serve him in sincerity and in faithfulness. Put away the gods that your fathers served beyond the River and in Egypt, and serve the LORD. And if it is evil in your eyes to serve the LORD, choose this day whom you will serve, whether the gods your fathers served in the region beyond the River, or the gods of the Amorites in whose land you dwell. But as for me and my house, we will serve the LORD. (Josh. 24:14–15)

But the people didn't follow the Lord. Or at least, not for very long. They made a show of worshipping the one true God while Joshua was still alive, but after their strong leader stepped off the scene, they immediately began to drift. They compromised and went after the idols of the surrounding tribes.

> Judges is the account of failure through compromise. Judges follows the downward spiral of the nation of Israel through repeated cycles of apostasy and defeat. Few books of the Bible show depravity in all its perversity and corruption as does the book of Judges. God was forced to chasten Israel over and over by allowing their adversaries to harass, oppress, and even enslave them.
>
> But as soon as Israel would repent and cry out for deliverance, God would send them a "judge" (*shopet* in the original) to bring them aid.... These judges were people raised up and empowered by God to meet specific crises in

Israel's history. There were fourteen judges in all … bridging the gap between Joshua's leadership and that of Israel's kings.[4]

This period of three hundred years was a series of one downward spiral after another. Things continued to get worse and worse for Israel as they ignored God and went after idols. Then they would be oppressed by their enemies and would finally cry out to the Lord. He would raise up a judge and deliver them. They would resume walking with the Lord but all too soon would start the downward cycle of idolatry all over again. And each time their sin and degradation got worse and worse.

This was the setting and background for the book of Boaz, and it's critical to understand just how bad things were in the nation at this time. Judges 21:25 is the last verse of the book of Judges, and it captures the spirit of the people and the outlook of a nation that was collapsing from within:

"In those days there was no king in Israel. Everyone did what was right in his own eyes."

This is the nation and the culture that Elimelech found himself living in. And it's very obvious that he bought into it with his whole heart. The name *Elimelech* means "God is my King." That may have been his name, but it sure didn't come out in his behavior or his actions. And the first sign that God *wasn't* his King had to do with his response to an economy in a tailspin.

Elimelech Lived in a Bad Economy

Ruth 1:1 states that "there was a famine in the land." Food, of course, is a scarce commodity in a famine. You've heard of the law of supply and demand. When there is little supply of food the demand goes up—and so does the price. And then everything goes up. Not only did the price of food go up, but the price of feeding a donkey or a camel went through the roof.

Now let's stop right here and ask a critical question.

Why was there famine in the land?

Do you want the short version? It all comes back to the providence of God. God created the world, and He sustains the world. He keeps the whole thing with His provision—or to put it another way, with His providence. Food is a gift that comes from the Lord. That's why it's a good idea to bow your head with your family before you eat a meal and thank the Lord for what's on the table.

Giving thanks to God before a meal isn't a game or a cute ritual. It should be a prayer that comes from the heart—because you know in your mind that the food wouldn't be there if God didn't oversee the entire process that got it to your table.

I said that I would give a short answer to the question why was there famine in the land. The problem in doing that is that the best answer to the question is found in Deuteronomy 28—and that's a fairly long chapter. Deuteronomy 28 is the chapter all about the blessings and curses that God said He would bring on His covenant nation, Israel.

May I make a suggestion to you? Over the next few paragraphs I'm going to lay out some of the verses in Deuteronomy 28. The temptation will be to skip over them. Don't do that—read them. Read them carefully and thoughtfully. If Elimelech had paid attention to these verses, it might have saved him from making the biggest mistake of his life. So with that in mind, let's look at the first fourteen verses that describe God's promise of blessing to His people:

> And it shall come to pass, if thou shalt hearken diligently
> unto the voice of the LORD thy God, to observe and to do
> all his commandments which I command thee this day, that
> the LORD thy God will set thee on high above all nations
> of the earth:

And all these blessings shall come on thee, and overtake thee, if thou shalt hearken unto the voice of the LORD thy God.

Blessed shalt thou be in the city, and blessed shalt thou be in the field.

Blessed shall be the fruit of thy body, and the fruit of thy ground, and the fruit of thy cattle, the increase of thy kine, and the flocks of thy sheep.

Blessed shall be thy basket and thy store.

Blessed shalt thou be when thou comest in, and blessed shalt thou be when thou goest out.

The LORD shall cause thine enemies that rise up against thee to be smitten before thy face: they shall come out against thee one way, and flee before thee seven ways.

The LORD shall command the blessing upon thee in thy storehouses, and in all that thou settest thine hand unto; and he shall bless thee in the land which the LORD thy God giveth thee.

The LORD shall establish thee an holy people unto himself, as he hath sworn unto thee, if thou shalt keep the commandments of the LORD thy God, and walk in his ways.

And all people of the earth shall see that thou art called by the name of the LORD; and they shall be afraid of thee.

And the LORD shall make thee plenteous in goods, in the fruit of thy body, and in the fruit of thy cattle, and in the fruit of thy ground, in the land which the LORD sware unto thy fathers to give thee.

The Lord shall open unto thee his good treasure, the heaven to give the rain unto thy land in his season, and to bless all the work of thine hand: and thou shalt lend unto many nations, and thou shalt not borrow.

And the LORD shall make thee the head, and not the tail; and thou shalt be above only, and thou shalt not be beneath; if that thou hearken unto the commandments of the LORD thy God, which I command thee this day, to observe and to do them:

And thou shalt not go aside from any of the words which I command thee this day, to the right hand, or to the left, to go after other gods to serve them. (Deut. 28:1–14 KJV)

The section of curses runs from verse 15 to verse 68.

That's fourteen verses of blessing and fifty-three verses of curses that God laid out before the people. I will simply quote the first nine verses of the curses. Why? Because they speak to the question of why Elimelech and his nation were experiencing famine:

But it shall come to pass, if thou wilt not hearken unto the voice of the LORD thy God, to observe to do all his commandments and his statutes which I command thee this day; that all these curses shall come upon thee, and overtake thee:

Cursed shalt thou be in the city, and cursed shalt thou be in the field.

Cursed shall be thy basket and thy store.

Cursed shall be the fruit of thy body, and the fruit of thy land, the increase of thy kine, and the flocks of thy sheep.

Cursed shalt thou be when thou comest in, and cursed shalt thou be when thou goest out.

The LORD shall send upon thee cursing, vexation, and rebuke, in all that thou settest thine hand unto for to do, until thou be destroyed, and until thou perish quickly; because of the wickedness of thy doings, whereby thou hast forsaken me.

The LORD shall make the pestilence cleave unto thee, until he have consumed thee from off the land, whither thou goest to possess it.

The LORD shall smite thee with a consumption, and with a fever, and with an inflammation, and with an extreme burning, and with the sword, and with blasting, and with mildew; and they shall pursue thee until thou perish.

And thy heaven that is over thy head shall be brass, and the earth that is under thee shall be iron.

The LORD shall make the rain of thy land powder and dust: from heaven shall it come down upon thee, until thou be destroyed. (Deut. 28:15–24 KJV)

The short answer is that they had famine in the land because they refused to obey the Lord and turned once again to the worship of idols.

I live in Texas, and just this week the governor of our state asked people to pray that God would send rain. At this writing, the state has had so many wildfires raging out of control that firefighters can't even begin to keep up. The farmers are fighting drought, and the firefighters are fighting a seemingly hopeless battle to contain the fires, fueled as they are by high winds.

The only hope was to ask God to send rain. And we had a governor who was ready and willing to do that.

By the way, this is the driest year in Texas since the days of the Great Dust Bowl. I've lived here over twenty years and have never seen so little rain. But the governor asked the people to pray to the Lord—and within three days the rain showed up, and the fires were 80 percent contained. Now that's what you call the providence of God.

America in these days has a lot in common with the time of the Judges, when "every man does what is right in his own eyes." Even judges who are to rule impartially set aside the law and order to make law and implement their own personal political beliefs. Recently, one judge in California overturned the will of seven million Californians who had voted that marriage was between one man and one woman. After overturning the critical vote, that one federal judge resigned, announcing that he was a homosexual.

Historically in America, judges were expected to recuse themselves if they had a personal stake in a trial. But this federal judge didn't do so. Why? Because he was doing what was right in his own eyes.

That's just one illustration of where we are in this nation. In many ways, we are living in the book of Judges. It's a time when our wives and kids need us to be Boaz and not Elimelech.

America is in moral and spiritual decline—and your favorite candidate or political party isn't going to fix it. Why are we in decline? The answer is that God has given us over to reprobate minds. A reprobate mind is one that doesn't use reason or discernment. It suppresses truth instead of embracing truth—just as Israel did in the time of the Judges.

Romans 1:18 explains why America is in spiritual and moral decline. The broken economy, devastating unemployment, and gay marriage are just symptoms. The root cause for our rapid downward slide is found in that verse.

Romans 1 is to the New Testament Christians what Deuteronomy 28 was to the Old Testament believers in Israel. It's critical, and once again I would suggest that you read it carefully and thoughtfully. Here's the text, and it explains where we are—and why your family needs a Boaz, and not an Elimelech, right now:

> For the wrath of God is revealed from heaven against all
> ungodliness and unrighteousness of men, who hold the truth
> in unrighteousness;
> Because that which may be known of God is manifest
> in them; for God hath shewed it unto them.

For the invisible things of him from the creation of the world are clearly seen, being understood by the things that are made, even his eternal power and Godhead; so that they are without excuse:

Because that, when they knew God, they glorified him not as God, neither were thankful; but became vain in their imaginations, and their foolish heart was darkened.

Professing themselves to be wise, they became fools,

And changed the glory of the uncorruptible God into an image made like to corruptible man, and to birds, and fourfooted beasts, and creeping things.

Wherefore God also gave them up to uncleanness through the lusts of their own hearts, to dishonour their own bodies between themselves:

Who changed the truth of God into a lie, and worshipped and served the creature more than the Creator, who is blessed for ever. Amen.

For this cause God gave them up unto vile affections: for even their women did change the natural use into that which is against nature:

And likewise also the men, leaving the natural use of the woman, burned in their lust one toward another; men with men working that which is unseemly, and receiving in themselves that recompence of their error which was meet.

And even as they did not like to retain God in their knowledge, God gave them over to a reprobate mind, to do those things which are not convenient;

Being filled with all unrighteousness, fornication, wickedness, covetousness, maliciousness; full of envy, murder, debate, deceit, malignity; whisperers,

Backbiters, haters of God, despiteful, proud, boasters, inventors of evil things, disobedient to parents,

Without understanding, covenantbreakers, without natural affection, implacable, unmerciful:

Who knowing the judgment of God, that they which commit such things are worthy of death, not only do the same, but have pleasure in them that do them. (Rom. 1:18–32 KJV)

The time of the judges was a time of no truth, no law, and no absolutes. And we're right there with them. *It's all about what each man determines to be right for himself.* Self is the god, self is the judge, self is the idol, self is the problem. And when self is king instead of God being King, the inevitable result is lawlessness and narcissism. If it feels good, do it. If it's against the law, ignore the law and make up your own.

That's precisely what Elimelech did. He thought he could outrun and avoid God's discipline of famine by making a short-term move.

But it didn't quite turn out the way he intended.

Elimelech Made a Bad Plan

I don't usually tell a story that I told in a previous book, but I have to make an exception on this one. If you've read it already, forgive me. But I have to say it again, because it drives home a key principle about Elimelech's plan in a time of financial hardship.

Ron Wayne tries to get by each month by stretching his Social Security check and playing video poker at a casino in Nevada. He's seventy-six years old, and like a lot of people these days, he's feeling the pinch financially.

It's somewhat ironic, however, that he of all people would feel anything approaching a pinch.

After all, he is one of the founders of Apple.

When Apple was formed on April 1, 1976, Wayne signed the legal papers along with Steve Jobs and Steve Wozniak. Jobs and Wozniak each held 45 percent of the stock, and Ron Wayne had the other ten. Eleven days later he sold his shares for $800. On an impulse, he decided to get out of the infant corporation. Personal computers? Well, they probably wouldn't catch on, anyway.

So Roy Wayne took the $800 sure money and got out. But if he had held on … his stock today would be worth $22 billion.[5]

The old Kenny Rogers song says, "You got to know when to hold 'em, know when to fold 'em."

Elimelech made a bad decision based on the famine and the current economy in Bethlehem. Elimelech's name means "God is my King," but there is no indication that he consulted the King before he implemented his plan. Trying to escape the disastrous famine, he created an even bigger disaster for his family.

In a nutshell, Elimelech decided to fold 'em when the famine hit.

It would have been a better move to hold 'em.

Ecclesiastes 7:13–14 explains why:

> Consider the work of God: who can make straight what he has made crooked? In the day of prosperity be joyful, and in the day of adversity consider: God has made the one as well as the other, so that man may not find out anything that will be after him.

Elimelech refused to "consider" what God was doing in the time of adversity. All he could see was his bank account and the fact that the grocery store shelves were half empty. So he folded his cards and decided to outrun the adversity. His plan was simple: he would move from Bethlehem to Moab for a short time.

I should point out that Boaz also lived in Bethlehem during the same time of crisis and decided to stay. Why did he stay? Because he looked at the entire situation in the context of what God was doing in his life and in the life of his nation. In other words, he "considered" what God was doing through His providential famine—and he decided that the prudent and wise move was to stay put. That requires a little explanation, and we'll get to that in the next chapter.

But for right now let's make this point:

A. P. Giannini made his way *into* the city when crisis hit in order to lend a helping hand. Elimelech *cut out* on his village and extended family when life got tough. You tell me who was the better citizen.

Why didn't everyone else leave town when Elimelech did? It was because they knew it was the wrong thing to do. But as we will see, he went ahead and ran the red light that indicated STOP. He intended to "sojourn" in Moab until the famine played itself out in Bethlehem.

A sojourn is a short stay.

He certainly never intended to end up buried in Moab.

Elimelech's plan was flawed at its very root, because he neglected to even consider the purpose of God in his life. For that reason, his brief sojourn turned into a ten-year hellhole of one disaster after another for him and his family.

Elimelech apparently never considered that his plans could go up in smoke. He was too busy trying to hedge his bets and outsmart what God was doing in his life and in the life of his people. He wouldn't give up his idols of personal peace and affluence—and that's why he was making the move. Things were looking a lot better economically in Moab than in Bethlehem. So on an impulse, he decided to load up the U-Haul. He wasn't walking by faith—he was walking by sight. In fact, there's no indication at all that he was a man of faith—and we will see that very clearly in the next chapter. For now, it's safe to say that he was one of those men who was just too smart for his own good.

I know, I know.

I may be reading just a little too much into this guy's attitude. But isn't it possible—or even probable—that Elimelech viewed himself as just a little more savvy than the average Joes who were slugging it out every day in the midst of famine, trying to find a way to survive and take care of their families? That wasn't for him—he was headed for Moab, the land of opportunity.

Don't misunderstand—there are times when it's perfectly legitimate to make a move to improve the lot of your family. But as we will see in the next chapter, this was an illegitimate move that Elimelech never should have made. But he made it anyway because he was apparently convinced that God's truth and commands didn't apply to him.

Elimelech may have had a very high view of himself, but God didn't. In Jeremiah 9:23–24, the Lord made this statement about men who are wise in their own eyes and view themselves a little higher than the poor saps around them:

> Thus says the LORD: "Let not the wise man boast in his wisdom, let not the mighty man boast in his might, let not the rich man boast in his riches, but let him who boasts boast in this, that he understands and knows me, that I am the LORD who practices steadfast love, justice, and righteousness in the earth. For in these things I delight, declares the LORD."

As one looks carefully at the life of Elimelech, there is virtually no evidence that he truly knew God. He may have been externally religious, but there was nothing of God in his soul. It was the insightful seventeenth-century pastor Thomas Watson who said:

> The dew lies on the leaf but the sap is hidden in the root.
> The moralist's religion is all in the leaf; it consists only in

the externals, but godliness is a holy sap which is rooted in the soul.… There is a great deal of difference between a stake in the hedge and a tree in the garden. A stake rots and moulders, but a tree, having life in it, abides and flourishes. When godliness has taken root in the soul, it abides to eternity; "his seed remains in Him" (1 John 3:9).[6]

The difference between Elimelech and Boaz was the condition of their hearts. Think about it: They both lived on the same soil just blocks apart in the same little town of Bethlehem. But they had two completely different responses to the very same difficulties and economic hardships of life.

We are living in the same kind of days that Elimelech and Boaz lived in. And that's why this book is going to focus on the two different paths these men took as they responded to bad times in a bad economy.

It comes down to this. Each man reading this has to decide before the Lord: Will I take the path of Elimelech or the road of Boaz? And it's a choice that we make every day of our lives.

The Lord Jesus summed it up in Matthew 7:13–14:

Enter by the narrow gate. For the gate is wide and the way is easy that leads to destruction, and those who enter by it are many. For the gate is narrow and the way is hard that leads to life, and those who find it are few.

Elimelech took the easy path—the wide road, the quick fix—and it led him to destruction. Boaz, on the other hand, took the hard way and went through the narrow gate, and it led to a life that he never imagined. The fact is you and I have both roads staring us in the face every morning when we get out of bed and take that first sip of coffee.

Which road will you take today? Not which road did you choose yesterday or ten years ago—what are you going to do *today*? Elimelech just continued to make wrong choices. Without question he had many opportunities to take the right course, but he never did.

It's too late now for Elimelech, but it's not too late for you. Regardless of the path you have been on, today is the day of salvation. Turn from your old way of life and turn to the Lord Jesus Christ. He is the great Savior, and He is there for you the moment you call upon Him:

> If you confess with your mouth that Jesus is Lord and believe in your heart that God raised him from the dead, you will be saved. For with the heart one believes and is justified, and with the mouth one confesses and is saved. (Rom. 10:9–10)

When the Lord Jesus Christ brings about His supernatural change deep inside our hearts and souls, He changes us from the inside out. And that's when you become a man who can break free from the foolishness of a self-centered life and can be depended on to serve God by serving others.

That's the Boaz heart and spirit. And it originates in the Lord Jesus Christ. Only He can make that change in our lives. By His power and grace, He begins the process of turning us into godly men who can be counted on when life falls apart.

Peter Marshall, the gifted pastor and first chaplain of the Senate once said:

> Once and for all, we must put out of our minds that the purpose of life here is to enjoy ourselves…. That is not what life is about. You were put here for a purpose, and that purpose is not related to superficial pleasures…. You do not have a right to happiness. You have a right to nothing.[7]

And that realization will bring the greatest happiness you can possibly imagine.

Boaz got that.
Elimelech never did.
Be a Boaz.

A Boaz Man reveals his true character in a crisis.

CHAPTER THREE

AREA 51

"Passion does not compensate for ignorance."
—Samuel Chadwick

It's the largest military base in the world. But even though it's located in the USA, in the state of Nevada, very few people will ever see it. In fact, from its very inception, great efforts have been made to keep it a secret. Annie Jacobsen's book on the history of Area 51 reveals:

> Area 51 is the nation's most secret domestic military facility. It is located in the high desert of southern Nevada, seventy-five miles north of Las Vegas. Its facilities have been constructed over the past sixty years around a flat

dry lakebed called Groom Lake. The U.S. government has never admitted it exists.[1]

Although every imaginable effort has been put forth to keep Area 51 under wraps, it's probably the most famous military base on earth.

Key to understanding Area 51 is knowing that it sits inside the largest government-controlled land parcel in the United States, the Nevada Test and Training Range. Encompassing 4,687 square miles, this area is just a little smaller than the state of Connecticut—three times the size of Rhode Island, and more than twice as big as Delaware. Set inside this enormous expanse is a smaller parcel of land, 1,350 square miles, called the Nevada Test Site, the only facility like it in the continental United States.[2]

Back in 1951, the United States tested nuclear weapons on this site; 105 nuclear weapons were exploded above ground, and another 828 were exploded deep beneath the earth in special tunnels and caverns.

Five miles northeast of the Nevada Test Site is Area 51. Everything that has taken place on this super-secret base and everything that takes place to this day remains highly classified. Only two projects related to Area 51 have ever been declassified by the CIA: The first was the U-2 spy plane, and the second was the A-12 Oxcart spy plane.

Now all of this might be very interesting, but what in the world does it have to do with the book of Boaz? Hold on for a minute or two, and I'll show you its relevance.

Forbidden Territory

Last week I found myself ready to board a plane in Chicago with nothing to read. I did a quick pass through the bookstore, eyeing the shelves and automatically rejecting just about everything I saw. (Would I have to resort to reading one of those generic airline magazines?) Then, with time running out before my flight, my eyes fell on the cover of a large and somewhat sinister-looking book by someone named Annie Jacobsen. The title on the book was *Area 51: An Uncensored History of America's Top Secret Military Base.*

I bought it and found myself with reading material that kept me turning pages for the rest of my journey and beyond. It's not a book of fiction—even though it reads like a Tom Clancy novel. Jacobsen actually interviewed nineteen men who served on the base for decades and couldn't tell anyone—not even their families—where they worked or what they did.

Everyone who worked at Area 51 had a cover story. These men were all between the ages of seventy-five and ninety-two, and she was able to do extensive sit-down interviews with each of them.

In addition, she interviewed fifty-five military and intelligence officers, pilots, scientists, and engineers who were all deeply involved with the Nevada base. All of these men were able to speak of Area 51 for the first time, because the CIA had declassified their projects, after twenty years.

Area 51 was a place of secrets, and it served to protect the United States by doing everything possible to develop weapons and technology that would enable us to spy on, attack, and destroy our enemies. Nuclear weapons, the U-2 spy plane that flew over Russia, stealth bombers, and our advanced drones that to this day search out and destroy members of Al Qaeda have all been secrets of Area 51. Each of these, however, started out as "black operations"—the most carefully guarded of military secrets. And that was and is the specialty of Area 51.

Access to this highly sensitive area isn't allowed unless you've been given a top security clearance. Upon entering Area 51—and this by special invitation only—one must sign an oath of secrecy. A worker on his first day at Area 51 had to sign away his constitutional rights and agree to have his home telephone bugged. Area 51 is incredibly remote and can't be reached by road. The airspace over the base is known as "The Box," and all pilots, civilian and military, are forbidden to enter its airspace.

In other words, with just a few exceptions, Area 51 is forbidden territory to every citizen of the United States of America.

Elimelech and Area 51

So you remember Elimelech, right?

Elimelech was a Hebrew living in the small village of Bethlehem, just about five miles south of Jerusalem. And when the famine hit, Elimelech decided to box up his stuff, pack up his wife and kids, and move about fifty miles to the southeast to a place called Moab, where he hoped to escape the famine.

No big deal, right?

Actually, it was a big deal. A huge deal.

To a Hebrew, Moab was Area 51. It was absolutely, categorically, off-limits. Elimelech knew this but shrugged his shoulders and went anyway.

This wasn't moving from Sacramento to Phoenix or Nashville to Orlando. This wasn't a normal kind of move that families make all the time to take new jobs; this was an attempt to outrun the judgment and hand of the Lord. This guy could have relocated to some other area within the nation of Israel, and it would have been fine. But he had it in his head to make a run to the forbidden space of Moab.

The move from Bethlehem to Moab was flat-out disobedience and rebellion to the revealed will of God. And by making this foolish and impulsive move, Elimelech put himself in harm's way and invited the discipline and judgment of God upon his life.

Once again, Matthew Henry hit the nail on the head:

> I see not how his removal into the country of Moab, upon this occasion, could be justified.... It is an evidence of a discontented, distrustful, unstable spirit, to be weary of the place in which God has set us, and to be leaving it immediately whenever we meet with any uneasiness or inconvenience in it. Or, if he would remove, why to the country of Moab.... If he had that zeal for God and had affection for his brethren which became an Israelite, he would not have persuaded himself so easily to go and sojourn among Moabites.[3]

Meanwhile, back in Bethlehem, the man named Boaz looked the famine square in the eye—and stayed put. Squaring his shoulders and tightening his belt, he made up his mind to ride out the hard times, trusting in the goodness of the God of Israel.

Bethlehem was, and is today, a very small town. Back in the day of Boaz, it was nothing more than a small village. At that time, Bethlehem was in an incredibly fertile agricultural region. Its very name means "the house of bread." It was in an area of prime land with timely rains that yielded legendary harvests. Bread was never hard to find in Bethlehem because of the amazing yield per acre.

And then the Lord sent famine on Bethlehem, and suddenly there was very little yield in the fields. The house of bread had almost run out of bread, but not quite.

The famine, of course, affected everyone. Boaz was just as impacted as Elimelech. Every family man was concerned for his family, but as far as we know, only Elimelech bolted for Moab. The other guys stayed put and rode out the famine.

Now remember, this was a period of history we now know as "the cycle of judges." Over and over again, Israel kept turning away from the Lord, inviting God's judgment upon their land. This was one of those times. And what was the purpose of God's judgment? To cause His people to reconsider their ways and turn back to Him.

In other words, there was a vital life lesson to be learned.

Trusting God in the Hard Times

God always has a remnant of people who love and serve Him with their whole hearts. Boaz was in that group. But he had to go through the famine and the economic hard times just like everyone else. This was a time for him to walk by faith, trusting in the Lord to fulfill His promises of provision. Boaz didn't run for the border when the going got tough. He stayed at his assigned post and remained faithful.

Boaz knew in his heart that if Bethlehem had been "the house of bread" once, in God's providence, it would be again.

But Elimelech, who lived just down the street in a gated community, refused to learn the lesson. He refused to turn his heart to the Lord and repent of his sin. He decided that he was smart enough to outrun and out-plan the judgment of God. At least that's how he viewed himself. But things didn't quite turn out the way that he envisioned.

I like the observation of Gary Phillips on Elimelech's move: "Two wrongs were involved here; he abandoned God's promised land, and he went to the land of God's enemies."[4]

This was one of the stupidest decisions ever recorded in the pages of the Bible. Elimelech could not have picked a worse place to move his family. He was undoubtedly afraid that he wouldn't be able to keep food on the table. But instead of turning to the Lord as his Provider and asking for His help, he willfully and defiantly ignored everything that God had said and moved his family to the cesspool of Moab.

Here's a quick rundown of Moab and why it was the Area 51 to the Jews.

Why Moab Was Off-Limits

Do you remember Lot and his family fleeing the destruction of Sodom and Gomorrah? The story is recorded in Genesis 19. They were told to flee the city *and not look back*. But then Lot's wife decided she was the exception to the rule and looked back. She was turned into a pillar of salt (God is able to do such a thing if He so chooses). Lot was then left with his two daughters, and together they fled to the caves surrounding the Dead Sea.

Soon thereafter, the two girls got their father drunk and had sexual intercourse with him, thinking that this gross sin was the only way that they would ever have children. The son of Lot and his oldest daughter was named Moab: "The firstborn bore a son and called his name Moab. He is the father of the Moabites to this day" (Gen. 19:37).

When Moses was leading the children of Israel out of Egypt into the Promised Land, they had to cross the land of the Moabites. They asked for permission to pass through, but the king of Moab flatly refused to grant them permission. In fact, Balak the king hired Balaam to actually curse Israel as they headed for the new land (Num. 22–24). Then in Numbers 25, the Moabite women seduced the men of Israel and turned them to Baal worship.

The false god that was favored most by the Moabites was Chemosh (Num. 21:29). Scripture called this monstrosity "detestable" and an "abomination" (1 Kings 11:7; 2 Kings 23:13 NASB). When a Moabite man was desperate for the help of Chemosh, it was a common practice for him to sacrifice one of his children to this demonic god (2 Kings 3:26–27).

And this is the land—the land of Chemosh—that Elimelech of Bethlehem thought would be an improvement for him and his family.

Here was a Hebrew male who had absolutely no relationship to the living God of Israel. His name, "God is my King," was simply a lie. Elimelech was the king of his own life, and it's certain that the Lord wasn't.

Iain Duguid expanded on Elimelech's state of mind:

There was no king in Elimelech's life, and therefore, like so many others in the days when the judges ruled, he chose to do what was best in his own eyes. Instead of following the path of repentance and faith, trusting the Lord to provide for his needs, he moved to follow what seemed to be the best prospects of supporting his family, humanly speaking. He chose the road to Moab.[5]

It was the very worst road he could have taken, and he took it with full knowledge of what he was doing. It would prove to be the most devastating decision of his entire life.

If you had asked him about his decision while he was backing up the moving van to his front door in Bethlehem, he might have said, "Really, it's no problem. This is just a short-term thing. I'll be back." You see, he planned on a brief stay in enemy territory until things got better at home.

He never planned on dying in Moab.

And he certainly never foresaw his two boys dying in Moab.

That sojourn—his own short-term plan to get around the economic difficulties at home—would wind up lasting *ten years*. Elimelech's cleverly designed plan to outrun the famine went down in flames and left his wife, Naomi, and his two widowed daughters-in-law in dire straits.

This is the backdrop of the book of Ruth that so many readers, students, and preachers just vault right over. But I don't want to leap over these short verses on Elimelech, because they are so full of lessons for those of us today who are leading families in tough economic times.

Now here's a question. It's obvious that Elimelech wasn't a true follower of the Lord. But what about a man who does know Christ as his Savior? In other words, are there any lessons out of Elimelech's life for those of us who do want to know the Lord and walk with Him?

The answer to that is yes.

Have you ever gotten ahead of the Lord? Have you ever made a decision that you look back on now and you can't believe how stupid you were? Have you ever charted a course that proved to be a complete and total failure?

Then join the club.

I happen to be a member of this club. In fact, you might say I'm a platinum member—a level of membership reserved for guys who have done some incredibly stupid things.

I'll be honest with you. Although I've known the Lord since I was seven years old, I've always had an Elimelech streak in me. What I mean by that is that I have a very strong bent toward making strategies and mapping out plans in my own mind and then moving on them before the Lord gives the green light. And this is a bent in me that doesn't lend itself to being a submitted follower of the Lord.

So the Lord takes His men who suffer from this bent and carefully and skillfully begins to cut it out of our lives.

It's what I call the Elimelech procedure.

It's sort of like a prostate surgery without anesthesia—the Lord's very unique way of keeping you out of Area 51. It's His method and strong medicine to keep you from wandering over to Moab.

The Elimelech procedure will save your life, turning you into a man who learns to say, "Not my will, but Yours be done." And that's exactly where He wants us to be. That's the Boaz Man.

By the way, I should mention that I've had to go through the Elimelech procedure several times. Allow me to relate just one such experience. In fact, it was the one that shocked me the most and hurt more than I ever thought possible.

Finding the Right Slot

As the years go by, every man learns more about himself and how he's wired. It took me just about forty years to figure out that I really didn't have the gifts to be a pastor.

Now don't get me wrong. I love to preach, but *pastoring* is a lot more than standing behind a pulpit and preaching a sermon. Pastoring a church means juggling about six or seven balls every waking hour of your life.

A pastor has to be able to multitask.

And therein is my problem.

I can handle only two balls in the air at the same time. And when someone throws a third ball at me, my stress level shoots up exponentially.

I don't mean to bore you with those details, but it's a key component that I needed to learn about myself. It also explains what I'm about to tell you. And yes, it all fits into the Elimelech procedure.

I pastored my first church at the age of twenty-eight. Let's just say that the people in that small church were somewhat desperate when I first came around. I think we had somewhere around fifty-eight people the first Sunday I was there. I was young, highly ambitious, and wanted to make a mark and grow that little church into a big church. That was the driving force of my life, and I thought about it pretty much all the time.

Like every waking hour.

I was hyperfocused on achieving that goal. The problem was that I really didn't have the gifts to pull it off. The church began to grow, and for that I was thankful. But when a church grows, you have to hire staff and give them direction. Now, at the age of sixty-one, I can tell you that the two balls I'm most comfortable with are preaching and writing. And for the most part, that's been my twin focus over the last twenty years. When I was in my first church, however, I thought I had the ability to juggle a lot of balls—but I really didn't. And the more I had to juggle, the more stretched and stressed I became. Yes, by God's grace the church continued to grow, but the more it grew, the more it needed oversight and attention. There were so many balls in the air that I began to lose count of them.

Suddenly, I was having trouble sleeping at night. I couldn't turn off my mind, thinking about what I had to do the next day. Most of the stuff on my list for the present day didn't get done and had to be shifted to the next day—along with the new stuff for the new day. It was snowballing on me. I knew I needed to hire some staff but wasn't even sure what I needed.

You can see where this is going. Let's just say that when I got to the two-year mark, our little church had experienced a very gratifying level of growth, compared to where we were when we started. But here was the rub. I was out of gas—mentally, emotionally, physically, you name it.

To use the familiar term, I was burned out.

Years later I had a very insightful session with a ministry consultant who demonstrated to me that I lived my life in two-year increments. Not everyone does that, but I do. I can work hard for two years on a project—but when I hit two years *and one day*, I'm done. There's nothing left in the tank. That's pretty much true to form for me. After two years, I'm energized by a new project, like starting another book. But I didn't know any of this about myself back then.

All I knew was that I was pretty much out of gas.

Yes, I kept pushing and working hard, but I had lost all enthusiasm and motivation. It was like metal on metal. I loved to preach, but gathering energy to prepare for next week's sermon was like pulling teeth. I prepared, studied, and read, but I was running on fumes. Mary, my wife, knew it and I knew it, but no one else knew it.

I pushed hard for another year. But somewhere during that year I began to feel guilty for taking a paycheck. I was still doing my job, but I had no enthusiasm or energy. I was worn out and didn't know why. I felt like a guy who was totally spent from running a marathon but then has to get up every morning and run another marathon. That's not how it really was, but it was how I felt each day.

If you ever find yourself in this position—fatigued, exhausted, and emotionally drained—you need to remember that this is *not* the ideal time to be making major life decisions. But that's exactly what I did. I pulled an Elimelech, and I didn't even know who Elimelech was.

Somewhat abruptly, I up and resigned from this growing, healthy little church that I had pastored. The people hadn't seen this coming and were blindsided by my announcement. Stunned. To be candid, I didn't do a very good job of explaining my reasons to the congregation. In my heart of hearts, I felt guilty because I was completely out of energy and could no longer throw myself into the work. I wanted to function at a 100 percent energy level but could manage only about 10 percent … on a good day.

So I quit.

Now you must be thinking that that was a pretty stupid move, and you would be right in that observation.

There were other things I could have and should have done to remedy that situation, short of running out the back door (we'll look at those principles in the next chapter). But I didn't. I was young, I was stupid, and I was apparently not very teachable. So the Lord allowed me to Elimelech myself. I didn't realize it at the time, but I was about to do prostate surgery on myself without anesthesia. As a result, it was going to be a rough and highly uncomfortable ride for the next twelve months.

Nevertheless, I would learn some very valuable lessons in those months that are still with me to this day. As a matter of fact, I was reviewing and reminding myself of those lessons this very morning.

Did I know and love the Lord back then? Yes, I did. I wasn't an unbeliever like Elimelech. But I still had a very strong tendency to rely on myself and my own plans. That was in me and it went very deep. It was a habitual dependence on myself and my own take on things rather than a dependence on the Lord.

Did I see that in my life at the time? I really didn't. I thought I was in submission to Him—and I was, to a certain level. But He wanted to take me to the next level of trust in Him. What I couldn't have known at the time was that the bottom was about to drop out of my life. And that I would be taking my family with me.

I alluded briefly to this story in a previous book, so I'll make this concise in case you've heard it before. I tell the story simply to illustrate that even if you have an Elimelech episode in your own life and take the wrong road,

God can still rescue you and put you back on course. That's because God not only is sovereign over our sin and has forgiven us in Christ Jesus but also is sovereign over our mistakes and foolish decisions. He can fix those; He really can. He can actually take the worst things that happen in our lives—even the ones that we've brought upon ourselves—and in His way and in His time, actually turn them for our good (Rom. 8:28).

Setting Yourself Up for Failure

Now that's my story, but each man reading this has his own story. I was a pastor, and you may be an architect, an IT guy, or a plumber. But no matter what kind of work we do, we all have the same reaction when our self-made plans run into a brick wall.

We get depressed.

I'm not an expert on depression, but I'm somewhat familiar with it. When I Elimeleched myself, hit the wall, and saw my plans go up in flames, I went into a deep, two-year depression.

This was completely new turf for me. I've learned since that some depression can be traced back to a physical or chemical imbalance. My depression was from an imbalance of stupidity: I was more stupid than I was smart. To be more precise, I've also learned that depression can come from some kind of loss or blocked goals. My plan hadn't worked, and therefore it blocked all of my goals. And as a result, it brought a lot of financial hardship on my family, and we suffered a good deal of loss.

This just doesn't happen to guys in ministry ... does it?

Yes, truthfully it does.

I've also seen it happen to football coaches, attorneys, truck drivers, backhoe operators, and airline pilots. Depression can smack down *any* of us when our plans don't work, our goals get blocked, and our dumb moves result in great loss to our families.

Paul Tripp is a very wise and gifted biblical counselor. I was reading a piece he wrote about a particular form of depression that hits pastors—and sometimes causes them to run to Area 51.[6]

In his article, he referred to a pastor who, at the age of forty-five, walked into a board meeting and resigned. The guy was done with preaching, done with the church, and wanted nothing more than to escape his life and head in a new direction. Any direction.

Tripp then went into four ways that we set ourselves up for such a fall. He calls them "setups." It's not that someone else sets us up; we set ourselves up. We actually set ourselves up to become Elimelechs—and somehow don't see that immovable brick wall toward which we are speeding at a breakneck pace.

As I got into Tripp's insightful material, I thought to myself, *This doesn't just apply to pastors; it applies to any guy who knows the Lord and is trying to get through life.* It doesn't matter if you're a karate instructor, an editor, a city manager, or a mechanic. This stuff makes sense. It seems to me that each one of us could benefit from a quick evaluation of these setups. If you don't recognize and deal with these perils, you could unwittingly set yourself up to run off to Area 51.

Oh, and by the way, just to let you know, if after reading the setups that follow, you determine that all four apply to you—don't panic. He's got a great solution at the end of the list that will give you tremendous hope … and a way out.

Setup 1: Unrealistic Expectations

When I look back on my crisis in my first church, I can see that I took the bait on this one—hook, line, and sinker. From the time I walked in the door, I was determined to grow that little church into a big one.

Now, in hindsight, I think the Lord wanted to use that time primarily to grow *me* up, even as He used me to teach and lead that small group of believers.

Did I grasp that? I really didn't. I knew I had a long way to go, but I had no clue how much work the Lord needed to do in my heart and life to prepare me. If I had seen the growth I was hoping to see, it would have ruined me. There's no way I could have handled it. Did the church see some growth? Yes, and it was growth for which I should have been thankful. But I wanted more. I wanted big numbers. And that's where my expectations were unrealistic.

If you're in sales, it's easy to have unrealistic expectations. The same is true if you're building a business. Or here's another: marriage. We find the right girl, get married, and imagine that all of our expectations will be immediately fulfilled. But that's just not going to happen. Marriage is hard work, and it takes a good fifty or sixty years to get it right.

Unrealistic expectations are a subtle way of setting ourselves up for disappointment, discouragement, and even depression. So what do we do? Take a step back and get real. If you haven't jogged in five years, it's an unreal expectation to think you can run a marathon. That's just setting yourself up for failure.

Do you have a friend you can talk with at a real gut level? Get some time with him and talk about your expectations, and then ask for his feedback. When he gives it to you, don't just write it off. Evaluate it carefully. It could keep you from flipping out and going to Area 51.

Setup 2: Family Tensions

What Tripp has in mind here for pastors is their public life as opposed to their real-life struggles at home. If you have to keep up a front all of the time in public that you've got everything together at home, that's tough to keep up. The big one here is giving the impression that you have your work and your family responsibilities in balance.

Once again, that's not true for guys just in church ministry; that's a huge battle for all of us. Every guy I know struggles with balancing his family and his career. And I don't know anybody who has found and maintained the balance flawlessly. During my pastorate in that first church, I remember Mary asking me one night if we could go out and see a movie. I really didn't want to go. I had too much going on at church. In a very nice way, she reminded me that the two of us hadn't been out alone for months. As I thought about it, I realized that she was right. I was completely out of balance at home—and at my work. So I had to deal with my shortcomings as a husband. That seems like a small thing, but it could have become very serious if I had neglected to take the right steps.

The key to finding balance is losing it. That's how you learned to ride a bike. I remember my dad taking off the training wheels from my bike, and I was excited because I was seventeen. Actually, I was more like six or seven, but when he took them off, he ran alongside me with his hand on the back of the seat. I never knew when he was letting go, but I do know this: when I lost balance to the left, I would compensate to the right. That's how you learn balance. And I'm still learning it—aren't you? Our wives and kids need us to never stop learning.

I'm thinking of one man who is so absorbed in his own work that he has completely lost his own family. This man is solid in the Bible, but he is so blinded by selfish ambition that he blames everyone and everything for the condition of his family. It has been suggested to him by those who care for him that he has played a role in this by ignoring the needs of his family and being excessively harsh. He immediately denies any wrongdoing and merrily continues in his ministry efforts.

He's been in Area 51 for a long time.

If he doesn't open his eyes soon, he may never be able to leave.

Setup 3: Fear of Man

The fear of man is simply being afraid of what man can do to you. If you have a boss who gives you a bad review, and the fear of that review causes you to compromise in a place where you should stand firm, then that's the fear of man. A pastor who is preaching on an unpopular subject must teach what the verses in the Bible really mean. He can't slide by them, and he can't explain them away. He needs to carefully determine the meaning in its context and then preach it, regardless of how people will respond.

We need a greater fear of God than we do of man. Ultimately, you and I work for Jesus Christ, no matter what kind of work we do (Col. 3:23–24). You're not at work to preach (unless you're a preacher); you're there to do the job and do it right the first time. Work for the Lord, honor Him as best you know how, and leave to Him the responses of people in authority over you. He can turn their hearts whatever way He wishes. He runs them and He owns them. Your life and destiny aren't in their hands—they're in His hands.

The bottom line here? Quit trying to please people. Look to please God, do your job well, and then get the heck home and enjoy your wife and kids. I saw a good man lose his career *and* his family when he suddenly snapped and went half-crazy in his behavior. And the root cause was that he was a people pleaser. His entire existence was about pleasing others. He compromised his calling, his integrity, and his family by trying to keep everyone happy. And somewhere in his early forties, he snapped one night under the pressure and went straight into Area 51.

I haven't seen or heard from him since.

What a tragedy. He never trusted the power of God to deliver him from feeble men. And it drove him to ruin. The fear of the Lord is the beginning of wisdom. When you know that God controls all men by His power, it puts life in perspective and gives you wisdom. And that wisdom will keep you out of Area 51.

Setup 4: Kingdom Confusion

Here's the gist of my story in the early years. I wanted to build a big church, not just for God's glory but also for my own. But that just won't work.

I run into quite a few Christian guys who think that if they were "really sold out to the Lord," they would quit their careers and go into the ministry full time. They have somehow concluded that it would give God more glory if they were preachers instead of plumbers.

That's a crock. God has given you gifts—what are they? Use your gifts for His glory. The Lord gives us gifts and assigns us to our posts. If you're an incredible mechanic, then thank God for your gifts and inclinations. Don't try to be something you're not. You're good at fixing cars, you enjoy fixing cars, so fix the cars! And make those cars run to the glory of God. Charge an honest price for an honest job, and you'll never hurt for work. People will talk about you and send customers your way. And when you have success, give the glory to God, because He's the One who gave you the skill in the first place.

I've seen too many guys leave good careers because they wanted to be something they were never intended to be. Stick with your gifts. Francis Schaeffer used to say that there are no little people and no little places. If you try to be something you're not intended to be, you're going to get all stressed out, and at some point you'll probably get intoxicated with Area 51.

Be yourself and submit your will to Christ. *He* will make your life significant, without your trying to be someone or something you're not. Stay at home, do your work, take care of your family.

Don't be an Elimelech.

Solution: Run to Jesus

Instead of running to Area 51, run to the Lord Jesus. That's Paul Tripp's immediate advice, and it's very wise. If you're reading this and find yourself burned out and just about ready to buy a plane ticket to Area 51—stop. (Stop and give me fifty! My football coach used to say that.) What you need to do is stop what you're doing and just turn to the Lord. He knows your heart, your stress, and your confusion. And He knows that you don't see any way out.

But here's the deal. *He* is the way out. Run to Him, talk to Him, pour out your heart to Him. Believe me, He will take it from there. Just run to Him and pray Psalm 143:10–11 on your way:

Teach me to do your will,
    for you are my God!
Let your good Spirit lead me
    on level ground!

For your name's sake, O LORD, preserve my life!
    In your righteousness bring my soul out of trouble!

Elimelech, preoccupied as he was packing his U-Haul for Moab, never prayed that prayer.

Make sure that you do.

A Boaz Man rides out the hard times while trusting in the goodness of God.

CHAPTER FOUR

ROCK OR SAND

"As creatures, we have no right or reason to expect that at every point we shall be able to comprehend the wisdom of our Creator."
—J. I. Packer

The Navy SEALs train on the sand of Coronado Island so they can fight on the rocks of Afghanistan. In actuality, the SEALs can fight anywhere—sea, air, and land. That's how they came up with the acronym SEALs.

My friend Lawrence Aldredge gave me a heads-up on a great article in the *Wall Street Journal* called "The SEAL Sensibility," written by Navy SEAL Eric Greitens. It made me think about the parallels between the men who fail and the men who pass the rigorous SEAL training and Elimelech and Boaz.

The training to become a SEAL is pure torture. But there's a reason for it. Greitens put it like this:

> The pinnacle of SEAL training is known as Hell Week, a period of continuous tests and drills during which most classes sleep only a total of two to five hours.
>
> What kind of man makes it through Hell Week? That's hard to say. But I do know—generally—who won't make it. There are a dozen types that fail: The weight-lifting meatheads who think that that the size of their biceps is an indication of their strength, the kids covered in tattoos announcing to the world how tough they are, the preening leaders who don't want to get dirty, and the look-at-me former athletes who have always been told they are stars but have never been pushed beyond the envelope of their talent to the core of their character. In short, those who fail are the ones who focus on show. The vicious beauty of Hell Week is that you either survive or fail, you endure or you quit, you do—or you do not.
>
> Some men who seemed impossibly weak at the beginning of SEAL training—men who puked on runs and had trouble with pull-ups—made it. Some men who were skinny and short and whose teeth chattered just looking at the ocean also made it. Some men, who were visibly afraid, sometimes to the point of shaking, made it too.
>
> Almost all the men who survived possessed one common quality. Even in great pain, faced with the test of their lives, they had the ability to step outside of their own pain, put aside their own fear and ask: How can I help the guy next to me? They had more than the "fist" of courage and physical strength. They also had a heart large enough

to think about others, to dedicate themselves to a higher purpose.[1]

There it is—the Boaz attitude and spirit.

And Elimelech didn't have it.

When it came to famine and suffering, he looked for the nearest exit. He failed Hell Week. He was all show and no go. In Texas they have a term for that: Big hat, no cattle.

Boaz stayed the course and rode out the tough times, trusting in the Lord to get him through. Elimelech decided to outmaneuver God and head to Moab. In so doing, he was building his house on the sand.

Boaz stayed put and placed his confidence in the Lord to get him through the famine. He knew that Moab had managed to miss the famine and that the economy was smoking over there. But he didn't have a green light from the Lord. So he stayed in Bethlehem. That's what you call building on the rock.

It's All about the Foundation

In Matthew 7:24–27, the Lord Jesus closed off His powerful Sermon on the Mountain with these words:

> Therefore everyone who hears these words of mine and puts them into practice is like a wise man who built his house on the rock. The rain came down, the streams rose, and the winds blew and beat against that house; yet it did not fall, because it had its foundation on the rock. But everyone who hears these words of mine and does not put them into practice is like a foolish man who built his house on sand. The rain came down, the streams rose, and the winds blew

and beat against that house, and it fell with a great crash.
(NIV)

Boaz Men build on rock.

Elimelech Men just build and don't think ahead. Don't get me wrong. They do think ahead, but they don't think *far enough* ahead. They may think about health insurance, college tuitions, retirement, and even burial expenses. But here's the problem: When we die, we don't cease to exist. We live forever. Our bodies may be in the ground, but our souls—our essential *selves*, our minds, wills, and personalities—will never go out of existence.

Elimelech thought he was a cut above the other men who were staying put in Bethlehem. He had a plan to make a short-term move to Moab and ride out the hard times back home. I'm sure he was patting himself on the back for "thinking ahead."

But it was all sand.

And that's why it fell apart.

As we will soon see, building on the sand left his family in a horrific situation. But somehow that never dawned on him, even though he was a real smart guy—at least in his own mind. But the problem with smart guys or dumb guys or in-between guys is that none of us have any control whatsoever over our futures.

Building on the rock means that you trust God with your future. Building on the sand means that you think you can control your own future. Boaz built on rock. Elimelech built on sand. Boaz was wise and on point. Elimelech was unwise and off point

Elimelech reminds me of a man named Demas, whom Paul mentions in 2 Timothy 4:10: "For Demas, in love with this present world, has deserted me and gone to Thessalonica."

Both Elimelech and Demas deserted and went to Area 51. Loving the "good life" more than the Lord, each of them packed it in and made an escape: Elimelech to Moab, and Demas to Thessalonica.

That's not smart in the Old Testament or the New Testament. When you try to fly over the restricted airspace of Area 51, you always get shot down.

Elimelech's self-devised, short-term plan to eliminate adversity in his life resulted in three obituaries and three destitute women. He ignored completely the spirit of Ecclesiastes 7:13–14:

Consider the work of God:
who can make straight what he has made crooked?

In the day of prosperity be joyful, and in the day of adversity consider: God has made the one as well as the other, so that man may not find out anything that will be after him.

In adversity, Elimelech refused to consider the work of God and what the Lord was attempting to do in his life.

You may be thinking that this is what you have done. You conjured up a plan that you thought would bring relief, and it has blown up in your face. And now things are worse than before. You see a lot of Elimelech in you, and you're thinking that you've made an incredible mess of things. You may even imagine that things in your life have now veered absolutely out of control.

The truth is they may be out of *your* control, but they are not out of God's control. Your plans have crashed and burned in Area 51. But in all honesty, that's the very best thing that could have happened. God has a plan even when your plans go down in flames. Unfortunately, it often takes a complete and a total failure of our plans and dreams to get us to the point of surrendering to the plan of God. But that is the safest and wisest place that we could ever be.

When everything we have planned is going up in flames, that's the very time when we should be ready to listen to God and to submit to His plan. Someone has said that failure is the opportunity to begin again more intelligently.

Precisely.

And that's the purpose of this chapter.

In times of great economic pressure, there are some things that the Christian should and should not do. There are old ways of living that we should discard, and there are new truths we should pick up and apply.

Here are seven observations about what we should do in times of personal famine and economic hardship. Perhaps in these hard times you have realized that you have made an impulsive Elimelech move—or you are sensing a strong temptation to wander off across the no-man's-land into Area 51. These are principles, honed from the rock of God's Word, that can help you rebuild—even in the midst of famine.

Principle 1: If you find yourself out ahead of the Lord, or if you've veered away from Him, stop immediately and repent.

When Moses was leading the children of Israel in the wilderness, God led them in such a way that they couldn't miss it. He led them with a cloud by day and a pillar of fire by night. By the way, this also took care of their physical needs in the desert. In the summer months, that desert can get up to 130 degrees. And in the evening, deserts can turn bitter cold. So the cloud protected them from the sun during the day and the pillar of fire provided warmth at night. As God led them, He gave them central heat and air conditioning.

But note *how* He led them. When the cloud moved, they broke camp and went with it. When the cloud stayed put and hovered over them, they camped and waited. If you have gotten ahead of the Lord in your life, turn around and go back. Get back under His authority and get back under His mercy. It's never too late to turn around and run back to the Lord.

Think about this picture of God from the Old Testament. He told His unfaithful, wandering people: "All day long I have held out my hands to an obstinate people, who walk in ways not good, pursuing their own imaginations" (Isa. 65:2 NIV).

If you've been running away from Him, then turn around and go back. He's been holding out His arms, waiting for you to come home. That's what repentance really means; it's making a U-turn. Stop going the wrong direction, hang a U-turn, and go back. That's your first step to leaving the Elimelech error and becoming the Boaz Man who follows Christ.

The Lord wanted Elimelech to quit going his own way, make a 180 degree pivot, and head right back to the Lord God of Israel. Deuteronomy 30:2–3, 9 makes that abundantly clear. Here the Lord was speaking to everyone in Israel, including Elimelech:

> Return to the LORD your God … then the LORD your God
> will restore your fortunes and have compassion on you …
> the LORD your God will make you abundantly prosperous
> in all the work of your hand, in the fruit of your womb …
> and in the fruit of your ground.

But Elimelech was having none of it.

And he lived to regret it.

But it's not too late for you to hit the brakes and return to the Lord.

Principle 2: In hard times, stay at your post and learn the lessons.

John Newton, writer of the hymn "Amazing Grace," lived an extraordinary life. Newton' s life was a dramatic demonstration of the amazing grace of God, and he marveled at God's work that had saved him and put him on course to be pastor. He was a sailor, a sea captain of a slave ship, a sexual reprobate, and a man so vile that other sailors were afraid to stand close to him on a ship.

But then the Lord changed and regenerated him and made him alive in Christ Jesus. Through many providential events, the Lord continued to steer the steps of John Newton.

Newton's career as a captain of a slave ship was providentially interrupted when he became violently ill just hours before the ship was to sail. Since Newton was unable to get out of bed, another captain was called and the ship sailed out of the harbor. Within minutes, Newton's health was restored to him—and he never captained another ship again.

Did he fight that change in career and direction and use all of his influence to get another ship? No, he didn't. He and his wife sensed very strongly that the Lord was leading him in another direction. He immediately was offered a high-ranking position as surveyor of the tides. In essence, he became a harbormaster and was responsible for every ship that came in and out of the harbor. At the same time, he had a growing desire to grow in the Scriptures. He used his off hours from his new position to throw himself into the study of the Bible. He couldn't have done that in the middle of the ocean. So God changed his plans and kept him in port, and he adjusted accordingly. In other words, he stayed put and learned the lessons.

As he moved toward ordination, he had to wait for six long years before he was approved. Once again, he stayed put in the midst of disappointment and learned the lessons.

Finally, when he was accepted as pastor of a small congregation, he found out that his small salary would be cut by 25 percent and paid to the former pastor who had accepted a fully paid pastorate in another town. He soon found out that his life savings had been completely wiped out when the financial institution to which he had entrusted it went bankrupt.

Suddenly economic famine was upon him. Did he start looking around and putting out his résumé in hopes of pastoring a bigger church? No, he didn't take that course, because he had no clear leading to do so. He knew that trials were from the Lord and that his faith was being tested (James 1:2). So he stayed put and learned the lessons. In his own words he described his response to the bad financial news:

> Had advice today that my friend Joseph Manesty at Liverpool is bankrupt, so I suppose what I had in his hands is quite lost. It was not much, but it was my all. I repine not at this. The Lord has made him an instrument of much good to me in times past; and though creatures fail the Lord will not want means to give me what he sees necessary.[2]

Is it wrong to seek another job if the one you're in is unfulfilling or a dead-end street? No, not necessarily. If you can legitimately change your circumstances and you sense the Lord's plain leading with a clear conscience, then go ahead and put out the feelers in an appropriate way. But at the same time, make sure that you're being led to go and that you're not bolting just to bolt.

Does the Lord have lessons yet for you to learn in your present circumstances? Ask Him! He'll let you know in ways we'll discuss later in this chapter. But whatever you do, don't pull an Elimelech and race for the back door.

Trust me—I say that from experience.

Principle 3: In hard times, keep a godly support system.

When Elimelech left Bethlehem and went into Moab, he was flying blind and unprotected. First of all, he left the land that had been given to him and his family by divine distribution—the very inheritance of his fathers.

When the children of Israel entered the Promised Land, the promise that God had made to Abraham was fulfilled. The tribes were given vast sections of land, which they were to work and pass on from one generation to another. It was an inheritance from God to their fathers—and it was no light thing to walk away from it. Elimelech was choosing to walk away from the safety and support of his God, his family, and his extended national family.

Sinclair Ferguson explained why this was such a foolish move:

> For one thing, they are forsaking the only place on earth God has specifically given to his people, the place in which he has promised to bless them and provide for all of their needs. In the old covenant there were particular geographical spaces and times that God had designated as "holy." These were specific places where God promised to meet with his people. Eventually they formed a series of concentric circles: the Promised Land, the city of Jerusalem, The Temple and, at the centre, the Holy of Holies. The

Promised Land was the one place on earth where, whatever happened, you could be safe sheltering under the shadow of the Almighty (Psalm 91:1ff).[3]

Over the years two men have stood out to me because they have understood the importance of a godly support system. They lived in different states and didn't know each other. But I saw each of them go through a very similar decision-making process with their wives when they were offered significant corporate promotions.

After weeks of pondering and praying, each man turned down the promotion. In both cases, their fellow executives thought they had lost a mental tire on the corporate freeway. *"Promotions like these don't come along every day! You've got to strike while the iron's hot!"*

Each man, however, with full support of his spouse, turned down the respective promotion because of the healthy, Bible-believing church that their families were plugged into. Specifically, each one of their kids was happy and connected in strong ministries with godly friends and leaders. They knew that was an incredible godly support system, and they just couldn't see their way clear to pick up and move—just to climb the corporate ladder.

Before making a move that perhaps would have been best for them personally, they both stopped and considered the impact it would have on each member of the family. And because it wouldn't be best for the kids, these guys each turned away from a lucrative offer.

That's a Boaz move. That's the move of the man who is listening to the wisdom of the Lord Jesus Christ.

Back to My Elimelech Decision

In the last chapter I began to tell you about my Elimelech decision to resign from my first church. That was an unwise decision made in the midst of burnout, frustration, and guilt. Did I pray and ask the Lord to lead me? Yes, I did, but I made some mistakes in discerning His will that we will discuss shortly.

Suffice it to say, it was my plan and expectation that upon resigning from my church, I would soon be invited to pastor another church.

I really expected that to happen.

But it didn't.

Oh, I got calls from churches and even interviewed with them. In fact, there were seven calls … and seven visits … and seven rejections. None of them wanted me! This definitely wasn't going according to plan—my plan. But it was going according to the Lord's plan.

Listen to the wise words of John Newton: "It is indeed natural for us to wish and to plan, and it is merciful in the Lord to disappoint our plans."

Did you catch that? It's natural for us to make our plans, and it's a great mercy for the Lord to disappoint our plans. Are you kidding me? Disappointment is a mercy? I'm not sure I would have agreed with that statement when I was thirty—but now that I'm thirty-one years further down the trail, I agree with it completely.

How would John Newton know about disappointment? In his day he was one of the most famous pastors in England and a hymn writer who was known across the seas.

But do you recall that he had to wait on the Lord for six years before his desire to be a pastor was fulfilled? He had studied diligently, learned Greek and Hebrew, and done everything he could do academically to gain admission to ordination. But in the denominational system of his day, one man stood in his way. And this one bishop refused time and time again to consider Newton for ordination. Meanwhile, other men who were less qualified were being ordained right and left. Newton had the ugly stain on his record of being a captain of a slave ship; plus he was much too fervent about the Bible, and not at all involved in the denomination.

How frustrating this must have been for young John Newton. Year after year his desire to be a pastor grew, and year after year he was disappointed.

But he stayed at his assigned post and relied on his support system. He had his wife, his pastor, and his great friend George Whitefield. They sustained and encouraged him when it looked like all roads were closed to fulfilling his life's ambition. No doubt plans were made to persuade the senior bishop, but they never were successful. It was a season of bitter disappointment for John Newton. With that in mind, let's get back to his quote.

"It is indeed natural for us to wish and to plan, and it is merciful in the Lord to disappoint our plans and to cross our wishes. For we cannot be safe, much less happy, but in proportion as we are weaned from our own wills, and made simply desirous of being directed by His guidance."

I find it interesting that one of the reasons we must be weaned off our own will is that it isn't safe! Our own plans, sincere and well thought out as they might be, can lead us right into a swamp—or off the sheer edge of cliff. That's what happened to Elimelech. His short-term plan to relocate to Moab looked pretty good to him on paper. But the outcome of his own death and the death of his sons indicated it certainly wasn't a safe plan.

Newton then went on to talk about the necessity of being trained in the school of disappointment. That's how the Lord weans us off of what we want and on to what He wants. Newton continued:

> This truth (when we are enlightened by His Word) is sufficiently familiar ... but we seldom learn to reduce it to practice without being trained awhile in the school of disappointment. The schemes we form look so plausible and convenient that when they are broken, we are ready to say, What a pity! We try again, and with not better success; we are grieved, and perhaps angry, and plan out another, and so on; at length, in a course of time,

experience and observation begin to convince us that we are not more able than we are worthy to choose aright for ourselves.

Now do you see why it's a mercy for the Lord to disappoint our plans? Newton was right—we may have confidence in our abilities, but we flat out don't know what we're doing. Left to ourselves and our own schemes and dreams, we simply won't choose rightly. So the Lord steps in to frustrate and disappoint our flawed and possibly dangerous plans. Once we understand that we can't choose rightly without Him, we begin to learn a key lesson:

> Then the Lord's invitation to cast our cares upon Him, and His promise to take care of us, appear valuable; and when *we* have done planning, *His* plan in our favor gradually opens, and He does more and better for us that we either ask or think.[4]

That is precisely how the Lord works!
Isaiah 55:8–9 lays it right on the table:

For my thoughts are not your thoughts,
    neither are your ways my ways, declares the LORD.
For as the heavens are higher than the earth,
    so are my ways higher than your ways
    and my thoughts than your thoughts.

Are you in the place of disappointment because your plans have been shattered? I remember going into a deep depression that ultimately took me over two years to recover from—and it was because my carefully crafted plans had gone down in flames. No, I couldn't see it then, but, oh, how I can see it now, looking back to that time.

After nearly a year of being turned down by church after church, hitting financial famine, having to go back to my old summer truck-driving job to afford groceries, and watching Mary nearly die from a blood clot, I watched God gradually begin to open up His plan.

Two small churches asked me to consider pastoring them. One I dismissed immediately because it was too close geographically to my former church, and I didn't think I had any hope of turning it around. The people were very gracious, but, quite honestly, they were old. I was in my early thirties at the time, and the average age of that church had to be over seventy.

Nevertheless, this church—this one church—kept pursuing me. And I kept saying no. After nearly a year of incredible hardship, a second church in another state invited me to come. Frankly, the salary was very generous for a small church, and Mary and I considered it carefully. But we felt we should decline.

Not taking no for an answer, the church's leaders raised the salary by a crazy amount, offered to buy us a second car, and (get this) were going to give us the down payment for a house. Not loan us the down, *give* it to us.

I told them no. They were godly men who loved the Lord and His Word and had remarkable financial resources that enabled them to make such a generous offer. If I had accepted, my financial famine would have been immediately over. But in my heart I felt a very strong sense of being checked by the Lord. So I said no. I had made one disastrous Elimelech move already, and I wasn't going to make another.

Can I tell you what the deciding factor was? A very wise friend had told me just the week before that my family and I had been through so much together that we really needed to make sure we had a godly support system around us. We needed the close support of family and friends, because we were pretty beaten up.

Because of that counsel, Mary and I agreed to say no.

At that point, I made contact with the first church, the one I kept turning down time after time. (I had even told them I was going to that church in the other state.) What I didn't know was that they had held a special prayer meeting to ask the Lord to keep me from going to that other church. When I called them, they said they had been praying and waiting for my call. They wanted me to come. And so we did.

It was a smaller salary, but it was sufficient. It enabled us to stay close to our godly support system who helped us to heal up as I fought off depression and Mary recovered physically. But the Lord had another benefit in mind that I knew nothing about at the time.

I should tell you one more thing. It wasn't a high-pressure church. Most of the people were older, and I had hardly any counseling appointments. I would study to preach and meet with the leadership during the week, but that still left a lot of time that I hadn't had in my previous church. Quite frankly, I was a little bored and looking for something to challenge me in this small church.

Mary and I were talking one night, and she suggested that I take a couple of doctoral courses while I had some extra time. I really hadn't considered getting my doctorate, not seriously anyway, but I started to look around at a couple of seminary programs for pastors. I really liked the one that Dallas Seminary offered. A few weeks later I mentioned it to the men on the church board, to see if they would be okay with my taking a couple of classes.

That's when something happened that I never expected to happen. They got excited about that idea. Every one of them. I showed them the brochure on the program, and the classes, and the more they read, the more animated and encouraging they became. They agreed that I should go ahead and apply. Looking through the brochure at the required courses, they asked me if I could use some of that material in my preaching and teaching.

"Of course," I told them. That was a no-brainer.

Then they said something that shocked me. They were so convinced that I should enroll in the doctoral program that they offered to pay my tuition.

That about floored me.

It was all part of a providential link that God had in mind for me—a link that has ramifications even to this day, almost thirty years later. It was in that doctoral program that I did original research on over a thousand men around the nation—and that not only became the basis of my first book, *Point Man*, but it also launched me into speaking to men all over the nation.

I couldn't have planned that if I'd had a million years to think it through. But God had planned it a million years before I ever walked this earth. Actually, He planned it all before He created time, writing all of that down for me in eternity past.

For the last twenty years I have ministered full time to men. No, I don't pastor a church, but I have spoken in over six hundred churches in the last two decades. I don't have to juggle all the balls that most pastors have to juggle. I get to speak and write. That's two balls. And that's about it for guys like me.

In other words, God is good to dumb guys.

Especially when they surrender to His plan on His schedule.

He's got you covered. And most likely, He will use a godly support system as a part of His provision.

So if you have Elimeleched yourself by flying solo, land the plane. Get a bigger plane and fill it with godly friends and family who are on your team. They will be there for you. And the next time you start drifting into Area 51 airspace, they'll help you change course quickly.

And who knows? They might even take up a collection and send you back to school.

A Boaz Man refuses to run ahead of the Lord.

CHAPTER FIVE

KEEP CALM AND CARRY ON

"The claim of the gospel is not only that it can give us a quiet heart, but also that nothing else can do it."
—Martyn Lloyd-Jones

It was 1939—a bad time to live in London. World War II was about to ramp up, and there was, understandably, tremendous anxiety about the state of affairs. It was fully expected that Hitler would soon be sending his bombers over London to devastate the British into submission. And on September 7, 1940, day and night bombing became a fact of life in England.

What was next? Invasion? With the fall of France, how could Hitler's Nazi hordes be prevented from crossing the channel?

That was no idle concern. Within a year, Hitler would have forty divisions of his crack troops lined up across the English Channel, ready for the order to cross over and invade England.[1] England was a brave land, but the nation's leaders were understandably concerned about the morale of the people.

In response to this unprecedented situation, the Ministry of Information produced a poster and began to distribute it across London for posting. The background was the Union Jack, the flag of Great Britain. In bold letters over the background of the flag, the message was straight to the point: *Keep Calm and Carry On.*

In 1939, Dr. Martyn Lloyd-Jones agreed to join G. Campbell Morgan, the great Bible expositor, as copastor at Westminster Chapel in London. But within weeks of his move to the church from Wales, everything changed dramatically with the sudden onset of war.

People began to flee London as the bombing commenced. On September 25, a bomb hit Westminster Chapel and destroyed some of the educational space. It was providential that the damage had been so minimal. By October 1940, thirty-two churches in London had been destroyed and forty-seven seriously damaged.[2]

Services were constantly interrupted by air raid alerts. As it happened, the two pastors of Westminster Chapel had different responses to the sirens. The elder Campbell Morgan would immediately stop the service at the very first warning. However, when the younger Lloyd-Jones was in the pulpit, he would preach right through the first warnings and keep going until the attack was imminent.[3] Lloyd-Jones, while not reckless, had a tremendous trust in the sovereignty of God. He knew that many of the warnings came long before the attacks, so he just continued to preach until wisdom dictated an exit. In other words, he lived out the adage—keep calm and carry on.

Things soon got even worse in London. "For fifty-seven nights in succession, an average of two hundred German bombers were over London every night."[4]

The attendance at Westminster Chapel, as in other churches, continued to drop dramatically. Because of the destruction around Westminster and the blocked roads, it was very difficult to get to the chapel for services. When attendance dropped, so did the offerings. Salaries were cut, and austerity measures were taken. In a very real sense, famine had come to London, and it also visited the faithful Westminster Chapel. At one point, Lloyd-Jones wrote to his wife that the chapel was surviving on a day-to-day basis.

Famine and economic hardship had come to London, and God's people were not exempt from the difficulties. But Martyn Lloyd-Jones kept calm and carried on.

When the famine hit Bethlehem and brought about tremendous economic uncertainty, Boaz kept calm and carried on.

But Elimelech was cut from another bolt of cloth.

When the lean times hit his hometown of Bethlehem, Elimelech panicked. He didn't keep calm; he ditched his heritage and inheritance for so-called greener pastures. He didn't carry on; he walked away and went against the Lord God of Israel.

So let's get back to the principles that we must learn in times of famine—no matter if we are in Bethlehem, London, or your hometown.

Principle 4: In hard times, don't run to the enemy camp for relief.

Throughout the Bible, you see men doing exactly what Elimelech did in going to Moab. For some reason, it seems that our first inclination when we find ourselves in trouble is to go to the wrong place and the wrong people for relief.

One weekend I was teaching on Elimelech at a men's conference. One of the men was asked to give his testimony. He got up and said, "The fact is, I'm just like Elimelech. Just like Elimelech, I made a bad decision and decided to check out Moab. It actually looked pretty good to me over in Moab. I had some problems in my life, and I decided that my life would get better fast if I moved over to Moab. So I did. And I liked it so much that I bought a house."

That was a very creative way of describing his Elimelech plan that ended up in failure—and ultimately brought him back to the Lord.

King Jehoshaphat was one of the few good kings mentioned in the Bible, but when a great army threatened him, he emailed King Ahab up north in Israel to help him out. It was one of the great mistakes of his life. Ahab was a godless reprobate who had married Jezebel, a bloodthirsty, sexually deviant woman who introduced wicked Baal worship into the land of Israel. This was the couple who kept trying to kill the prophet Elijah.

In 2 Chronicles 17:1–6, King Jehoshaphat was described in remarkable terms:

> Jehoshaphat [Asa's] son succeeded him as king and strengthened himself against Israel. He stationed troops in all the fortified cities of Judah and put garrisons in Judah and in the towns of Ephraim that his father Asa had captured.
>
> The LORD was with Jehoshaphat because in his early years he walked in the ways his father David had followed. He did not consult the Baals but sought the God of his father and followed his commands rather than the practices of Israel. The LORD established the kingdom under his control; and all Judah brought gifts to Jehoshaphat, so that he had great wealth and honor. His heart was devoted to the ways of the LORD; furthermore, he removed the high places and the Asherah poles from Judah. (NIV)

This man was serious about following the Lord, and for the most part he did. In 2 Chronicles 20:32, Jehoshaphat was honored as a man who did what was right in the eyes of the Lord. And that was all true.

But he also had a streak of Elimelech in him.

Sometimes, when the going got rough, the king started looking not east toward Moab, but north toward Israel, the northern kingdom. And in those days, the northern tribes that comprised Israel were just as bad as Moab. When the nation of Israel split after Solomon's death, all of the kings of the north were wicked. There were a few good kings in the history of Judah, which was the southern kingdom, and Jehoshaphat was one of the greats.

Except for that Elimelech streak.

He went north to Israel, which at that time was Area 51, and made an alliance with Ahab by agreeing to marry his son into one of the worst families in recorded history. And all for the sake of "keeping the peace."

When Jehoshaphat, the godly king of Judah, was in dire straits, where did he go for relief? Right up north into Area 51, which in this case was the house of Ahab and Jezebel. It was an insane move by a godly man who had let himself become gripped with panic. What happened to him? He didn't keep calm and carry on—he forgot the Lord in a moment of great danger.

Check it out for yourself. Second Chronicles 17 lays out the godly and wise reforms instituted by Jehoshaphat in the nation that honored the Lord. Then in the very next chapter of 2 Chronicles, you can read of his utterly foolish alliance with Ahab—which very nearly cost him his life. He made another great move in chapter 19 by appointing godly justices throughout the land, who were to fear the Lord in their rulings. And then in chapter 20, he faced tremendous dangers from a military coalition that vastly outnumbered his own defenses.

The king woke up one morning to the news that an incredibly large military force was just hours away—ready to march into Jerusalem and smash his little nation. This time, however, Jehoshaphat didn't run to Area 51 or any other area for help—he turned completely to the Lord, as we see in 2 Chronicles 20:5–13:

> Then Jehoshaphat stood up in the assembly of Judah and Jerusalem at the temple of the LORD in the front of the new courtyard and said:

"O LORD, God of our fathers, are you not the God who is in heaven? You rule over all the kingdoms of the nations. Power and might are in your hand, and no one can withstand you. O our God, did you not drive out the inhabitants of this land before your people Israel and give it forever to the descendants of Abraham your friend? They have lived in it and have built in it a sanctuary for your Name, saying, 'If calamity comes upon us, whether the sword of judgment, or plague or famine, we will stand in your presence before this temple that bears your Name and will cry out to you in our distress, and you will hear us and save us.'

"But now here are men from Ammon, Moab and Mount Seir, whose territory you would not allow Israel to invade when they came from Egypt; so they turned away from them and did not destroy them. See how they are repaying us by coming to drive us out of the possession you gave us as an inheritance. O our God, will you not judge them? For we have no power to face this vast army that is attacking us. We do not know what to do, but our eyes are upon you."

All the men of Judah, with their wives and children and little ones, stood there before the LORD. (NIV)

The Lord's response to Jehoshaphat's utter and total trust is recorded in verse 15 (NASB): "Do not fear or be dismayed because of this great multitude, for the battle is not yours but God's."

In other words, when the king went to the Lord instead of the enemy camp to make an alliance, he was delivered by the Lord's strong arm. Not only did the Lord defeat their enemies, but "the dread of God was on all the kingdoms of the lands when they heard that the LORD had fought against the enemies of the Israel" (v. 29 NASB).

To quote the wise John Newton one more time: "If He be all-sufficient, and gives me liberty to call Him mine, why do I go a-begging to creatures for help?"[5]

You would think this would have sealed the lesson in Jehoshaphat's mind and heart, but it didn't. Before Jehoshaphat died, he went into another alliance with the enemy—and this time it was Ahab's son Ahaziah (2 Chron. 20:35–37). It was a wicked alliance, and the Lord destroyed the ships that the two of them had built together. In reality, Jehoshaphat never learned the lesson of 1 Corinthians 15:33: "Do not be deceived: 'Bad company ruins good morals.'"

I'm not dead yet, and presumably you aren't either. We've still got time to learn the lesson. So don't start looking for houses in Moab. Get the heck out of there and get back to the Lord. He's your Banker, your Defender, and your Sovereign Keeper.

Principle 5: In hard times, be content with daily bread.

Elimelech left Bethlehem, a place where there was normally a great surplus of bread. But during periods of famine, bread becomes scarce. Life becomes a matter of survival when the surplus is gone.

Let's not forget Boaz in this equation. He isn't mentioned in the opening chapter of Ruth, but he too lived in Bethlehem during the famine. By the time he showed up in chapter 2 (which we'll get to before long), the famine was over and everyone was excited about the barley harvest, which was then followed by the wheat harvest. I'm getting ahead of story at this point, but it's a necessary fast-forward. As we will see, Naomi and her daughter-in-law Ruth went back to Jerusalem because they heard that the famine was over and Bethlehem was again living up to its name as the house of bread.

The point is this: Boaz made it through the famine. How did he make it? He made it because God supplied what he needed on a daily basis.

I had lunch with a man who has a very strong walk with the Lord. He has been unusually successful in business and featured in several magazine articles. For purposes of confidentiality I will purposefully omit certain details—but suffice it to say that this man over the last three years has been in famine. He told me that the basic rules of his business model were all completely changed almost overnight when the banking crisis reared its head in 2008. Without warning the regulators changed the rules. And it nearly took down a lot of guys who had been playing by the rules.

In football, you have to gain ten yards to get a first down. Imagine if that rule was suddenly changed without warning during a game so that *fifty* yards were required for a first down. And instead of four downs to get ten yards, the rules changed so that you had just two downs to get the fifty yards needed for a new set of downs. That, he explained to me, was essentially what had happened in his area of business expertise. The problem was that all of his business strategy was based on the original rules, and suddenly he found himself playing the game with not two legs but one—not two arms but one—and he was required to wear a blindfold. Almost overnight, the business that he had spent all of his life building was seriously weakened, and it was difficult to find a pulse.

As he told me this story, he reached to the middle of our table, grabbed the salt shaker and gradually started moving it to the edge of the table. Finally, he had the salt shaker right on the edge, so that two-thirds of it was on the table, but the other third was over the edge, hanging in mid-air. Then he looked at me and said, "This is where the Lord has had me every day for the last three years. I'm right on the edge almost every day. And just as I get to the point where gravity is going to take the salt shaker over the edge, the Lord will do something to rescue me and barely pull me back. Once in the last three years, He pulled me back about two feet from the edge. But over the last six months I've watched myself creeping ever closer back to the edge."

Taking the salt shaker and moving it about an inch from the edge, he said, "That's right about where He has me today."

During that two-hour lunch, he told me story after story of God's remarkable provision—at just the right time on just the right day—that kept him from going over the edge. He is a Boaz Man, living in the midst of famine, and he is making it day by day.

I imagine that's about where you are these days.

C. H. Spurgeon penned these words over a century ago:

> A daily portion is *all that a man really [needs]*. We do not need tomorrow's supplies; that day has not yet dawned, and its wants are as yet unborn.
>
> The experience that we may suffer in the month of June does not need to quenched in February, for we do not feel it yet; if we have enough for each day as the days arrive, we shall never know want. Sufficient for the day is *all that we can enjoy*. We cannot eat or drink or wear more than the day's supply of food and clothing; the more we have, the more we have to store, and we worry about it being stolen. One cane helps a traveler, but a bundle of sticks is a heavy burden. Enough is not only as good as a feast, but it is all that the glutton can truly enjoy. *That is all that we should expect*; a craving for more than this is ungrateful. When our Father does not give us more, we should be content with his daily allowance.[6]

That sort of cuts right across the grain of a lot of financial planning.

Is it good, wise, and prudent to have a financial plan? Of course it is. The Lord has told us He wants to be good stewards of our finances. But we aren't talking about "normal times"—we're looking at life in famine. In a famine everything dries up. The root cause of a famine is no rain. Drought comes before famine. There can be other factors that wipe out a crop or a harvest. Locusts can eat it, hail can destroy it, and boll weevils can ruin it. But the most brutal threat to a crop, especially a food crop, is long-term drought. And when there is no rain for year after year after year, the creeks dry up, the rivers shrink, and even the wells can go dry.

This is when the seven-year strategic financial planning is tossed out the window. In a deal like this you're not planning for retirement—you're trying to find enough food to feed your family for that day.

My dad has gone home to be with the Lord, but when he was a little boy, his father had days when he was literally asking God for food *that day* to feed his five kids. Your parents or grandparents went through the Great Depression, and more than likely they had days just like that.

But most of the readers of this book have never experienced that. Most of us have experienced decades and decades of unbridled prosperity. Sure, every once in a while there's been a glitch or two, but we haven't seen days like those in the 1930s.

For a lot of men, these are days of famine. They've lost their jobs and they're nearly exhausted from trying to find new ones. And the savings are about gone and the benefits are about to run out. That may not be your position today, but I guarantee that someone reading this is in that precise situation.

Like my friend, your salt shaker is right on the edge of the table, about to totter over the side and crash onto the concrete floor.

The Lord knows that's where you are, and He hasn't forgotten about you. As a matter of fact, He's got His eye on you. His eye has always been on you, just as His eye was on Grandpa when he needed to feed his five kids in the midst of famine.

You know what my grandpa did in those lean, hard years? He worked his tail off, and he trusted the promises of God. I know enough about him to know that he soaked his mind in the promises of Matthew 6.

Undoubtedly there were days when he would quote Philippians 4:6 to himself as he would visit the sick people of the church in which he pastored.

I'm sure that he would remind himself of Philippians 4:19 as he encouraged families who had lost their farms and homes—and he would be thankful that he had a roof for his kids to sleep under. At one time things were so tight financially that the only place he could afford was a small apartment above the volunteer fire department. My dad had more than one night as a little boy being awakened—frightened half to death—by a wailing siren and clanging bells suddenly erupting just ten feet under his bed. From that time on, every time my dad heard a fire truck siren, it took him back to those days living in the firehouse.

But they weren't sleeping outside, and they weren't in that little apartment for long. You do what you have to do in a famine—and you're thankful for the daily shelter and the daily bread.

God has promised to give daily bread to His people who call upon His name. That's either true or it's not. And there's nothing like a famine to test out a promise of God.

Whatever you do, don't go running off to Moab to ease the pain. Don't lie on your résumé to get a job. Don't falsify your expense account to pick up a few extra bucks. Stay clean, stay faithful, cry out to the Lord, and trust Him for your daily supply.

Principle 6: In hard times, keep a teachable spirit.

Since I have quoted John Newton so many times, one more isn't going to hurt. In that same letter that we previously looked at, Newton spoke to the necessity of being "trained awhile in the school of disappointment."

I wasn't a shining student during my college years. I wasn't all that interested in school in the first place, and there were many distractions when one was attending college in Southern California. My favorite hymn back in those days was "I wish they all could be California girls." And in my case, most of them were. Or on a few occasions, there were some from the Midwest and the South who were attending college in Southern California. I did what I could to make them feel welcome—but on to the point.

In all honesty, I had never been much into dating. I was too picky, and my friends who had girlfriends were always wrapped up in long conversations explaining themselves to their girlfriends. That just seemed like a waste of time to me. But my first year in Southern California there were so many beautiful girls at a nearby Christian college and in our church that I decided to change my philosophy. "Ye have not because ye ask not"—so I started asking girls out. I had a lot of fun, but I really tanked on school.

I was enrolled in college and the goal was to graduate with a good grade point average, but the lure of the perfume was strong. I will admit that I actually flunked two classes during that particular season. One of those classes I remember very clearly. First of all, I had absolutely no interest whatsoever in meteorology. And second, it never really dawned on me that I should make it a priority to attend that particular class. Quite honestly, I thought that I could figure some alternative way of getting through the course. In other words, how could I get away with skipping almost every class? This was another evidence of my Elimelech streak in those early years. Or to put it another way, it was another evidence of my incredible stupidity.

But here was my thinking. It was a huge class—close to a hundred students. And I didn't figure there was any way that professor was going to take roll in every class. How long would it take to go through a hundred names at the beginning of each class? But I honestly didn't know if he took roll every class, because when I did go to class, I showed up late. Sorry to admit to this, but it was the case back then. I knew a girl in the class who took copious notes and figured that I could cram off of her notes before the midterm and final. What I didn't figure on was that she had enough notes to fill the New York Public Library. My big hope was that this professor would grade on the curve, though I'm not sure he ever indicated anything of the sort. The guy was old school.

I didn't do real well on the midterm, but I was very optimistic about the final. I really had no reason to be optimistic; I just figured it would somehow work out—sort of like Elimelech going to Moab. Anyway, I flunked the class.

Long story short, about three years later there was a snag on my transcript. I was meeting with the registrar to try to come up with a solution (I won't bore you with the details). After a long discussion, the registrar suggested I go back and talk to the professor who had flunked me. Maybe he would allow me to do some additional papers or something of the sort to get enough credit to change my grade to passing. I had a very strong sense that there wasn't a snowball's chance in a microwave that this man would agree to any such proposal—even if it did come from the registrar's office.

As I walked over to the professor's office, I had the sense of a man walking to meet a firing squad. I kept thinking that someone was going to offer me a blindfold. I really didn't want to even go to his office, but then I thought, *He probably doesn't even remember me. He's had hundreds, maybe thousands of students since I was in his class. Besides, how would he remember me—I was never in class.*

I arrived outside of his office and knocked on his door, hoping he wouldn't be inside. To my regret, a voice said, "Come in." I opened the door, he turned in his chair away from his desk, saw me, and said, "Ahh, Mr. Farrar."

Right then, before I ever uttered a word, I knew I was dead in the water. And I was. This man was pure old school, and those are the best kind of professors. He told me that I didn't do the work so I wouldn't pass the class. As we wrapped up our short conversation, I told him that I agreed with him entirely and was sorry to have taken up his time. Three years later, I had learned at least enough to be humiliated and embarrassed at my failure—and I was angry with myself for even going into his office. It was a valuable and painful lesson.

Do you know what my root problem was in failing that class? I wasn't teachable. That's it. Did I have enough brains to pass that class? Yes. Could I have read the textbook with comprehension? Yes. Could I have taken my own notes and studied successfully to pass the midterm and final? Yes.

So why didn't I do those things?

I wasn't teachable.

I had to become teachable if I was going to pass any more classes. I had to become teachable if I was going to finish my degree, and then my master's, and finally complete a doctorate.

At some point you've got to become teachable.

Some twenty-five years ago I was speaking at a conference for Christian college students. Right before I was getting up to the third session, several young college girls came up to me and said, "Mr. Farrar, we have a very quick question for you because we know you're about to start the next session."

"Sure," I said. "What's the question?"

One of the girls spoke up for all of them. "We all hope to be married one day," she said. "What is the single most important trait we should look for in a Christian husband?"

I thought for a second and said, "Teachability. Look for a guy who is teachable. Every guy has flaws and weaknesses in spite of his strengths. But if he's teachable, if he's willing to learn the lessons and listen to the Lord—and listen to the opinion of his wife—that's a man who will grow into a godly man. But if he's not teachable, he'll never grow and he'll never mature. If a guy isn't teachable, *run*. But if he is, the Lord can do great things in his life."

So here's what it comes down to: we're in hard times and they may get harder. Are you teachable? You may think you are. But what would your wife say to that question? What would your closest friend say to that question? They know you best.

If you're teachable, you can learn the lessons and watch the Lord transform you, just like He changes a caterpillar into a butterfly. But if you're not teachable, you can forget about earning your wings, because you're going to stay a caterpillar.

Elimelech was a caterpillar to his dying day. He was never teachable and he never learned the lessons.

I've said it once and I'll say it again.

Be a Boaz.

And don't get worried if you've got a ways to go yet in the Christian life. If you're teachable, everything will be fine.

Keep calm and carry on.

A Boaz Man trusts the Lord for daily provision.

CHAPTER SIX

GOOD OUT OF BAD

"Bad decisions cannot be undone, but they can be redeemed."
—Erwin Lutzer

Israel Washburn Sr. and his wife, Martha, had a hard life. It was tough feeding their ten children on their small farm in Maine, far away from any settlements or towns. Israel ran a general store for the farmers in the area, and they all needed store credit to keep their farms going. The soil was rocky and not prone to producing bountiful crops. Farming in Maine in the 1830s was constant famine.

When Israel couldn't pay his bankers in Boston because the local farmers couldn't pay him, the bankers sent the sheriff to seize the assets of the store. The entire family was humiliated as the sheriff auctioned off all of the family's possessions to pay the bank. A kindly uncle stepped in to save the family farm, but the debts were so significant that the oldest children were shipped out to surrounding farms and towns to earn money to pay the debt.[1]

The children worked from sunup to sundown for months on end to earn twenty-five or thirty dollars to help their father. Finally, the debt was paid. The older boys were coming of age and one by one left home to make their way in the world. They were products of a loving family, remote isolation, biblical literacy, and hard, hard work. Each of them hoped to make a mark in the world and contribute to his family and neighbors.

The Washburn family, virtually unknown today, may have been the most famous family in America in the 1800s. And for good reason. All five of the brothers made their mark. Four of them were Congressmen—from four different states. Two of the four would be strongly considered for the Republican nomination for president and vice-president. They were either trusted advisors or bitter enemies of eight presidents of the United States. They led men in battle, served as foreign diplomats, built railroads and coal mines, and negotiated truces between warring nations.

One brother started a flour-making operation that produced a product called Gold Medal Flour. Another brother followed his lead and started another company called Pillsbury. Between the two of them, they owned the massive mills that provided flour to families across America—and even to the British Empire.

"The brothers redirected rivers and punched railroads across untracked prairies ... they built extravagant castles and humming factory complexes, as well as steamships and state-of-the-art scientific facilities."[2]

Thirty years after their father's humiliating bankruptcy, they built him a mansion on the family farm that stands to this day.

And through all of their successes and victories, they were never accused of financial impropriety or mishandling of funds. Each of the brothers had a moral compass that they adhered to all of their lives. They were men who were greatly respected, and they earned that respect by never wavering from the model their father set before them. Even in his business failure, the senior Washburn had been an honest and kind man, who had taught his boys how to handle the difficulties of life with courage and integrity.

Yes, the Washburns had indeed known bad times on the family farm in the remote wilderness of Maine. The boys were raised in hard times and learned the value of hard work.

Did any good come out of the bad?

Apparently so.

Hard Life, Hard Times

Ray Stedman, the Montana cowboy who pastored Peninsula Bible Church in California for so many years, used to say, "Resurrection power always works best in a graveyard."

We have taken pretty much half of this book to demonstrate that the self-generated plans of Elimelech died a long and painful death in the land of Moab. As we come to the next section of the story, Elimelech is dead and his two sons are dead, with their young wives left as widows. And Naomi, the woman who left Bethlehem with her husband, has buried the three men in her life.

> But Elimelech, the husband of Naomi, died, and she was left with her two sons. These took Moabite wives; the name of the one was Orpah and the name of the other Ruth. They lived there about ten years, and both Mahlon and Chilion died, so that the woman was left without her two sons and her husband. (Ruth 1:3–5)

It's a tragic story. The plans of Elimelech literally wound up in a graveyard. But God was about to bring good—unbelievably great good—out of the entire mess.

That's what resurrection power does. It takes our screwed-up, self-centered plans, kills them, and then God raises up an astonishing solution we could never have imagined.

Then she arose with her daughters-in-law that she might return from the land of Moab, for she had heard in the land of Moab that the LORD had visited His people in giving them food. So she departed from the place where she was, and her two daughters-in-law with her; and they went on the way to return to the land of Judah. And Naomi said to her two daughters-in-law, "Go, return each of you to her mother's house. May the LORD deal kindly with you as you have dealt with the dead and with me. May the LORD grant that you may find rest, each in the house of her husband." Then she kissed them, and they lifted up their voices and wept. And they said to her, "No, but we will surely return with you to your people." But Naomi said, "Return, my daughters. Why should you go with me? Have I yet sons in my womb, that they may be your husbands? Return, my daughters! Go, for I am too old to have a husband. If I said I have hope, if I should even have a husband tonight and also bear sons, would you therefore wait till they were grown? Would you therefore refrain from marrying? No, my daughters; for it is harder for me than for you, for the hand of the LORD has gone forth against me."

And they lifted up their voices and wept again; and Orpah kissed her mother-in-law, but Ruth clung to her.

Then she said, "Behold, your sister-in-law has gone back to her people and her gods; return after your sister-in-law." But Ruth said, "Do not urge me to leave you or turn back from following you; for where you go, I will go, and where you lodge, I will lodge. Your people shall be my people, and your God, my God. Where you die, I will die, and there I will be buried. Thus may the LORD do to me, and worse, if anything but death parts you and me." When she saw that she was determined to go with her, she said no more to her. (Ruth 1:6–18 NASB)

In 1662, all of the conservative, Bible-believing pastors in England were banished from the church. It was known as the Great Ejection. Overnight, these men lost their pulpits and their incomes. Because of their faithfulness to preach the gospel, they lost their ministries and their abilities to feed their families. Law forbade them to come within five miles of their churches. It was a time of intense persecution.

One of those banished pastors was Thomas Watson. Like his fellow pastors, Watson had lost his position and all of his possessions. In the process of enduring these things, he wrote a small book to encourage his fellow dispossessed pastors. I have worn out several copies of his book *All Things for Good*, which of course is based on Romans 8:28: *"And we know that for those who love God all things work together for good, for those who are called according to his purpose."*

The first chapter is titled "The Best Things Work for the Godly."

The second chapter is titled "The Worst Things Work for the Godly."

And in that second chapter he masterfully demonstrates how God takes the very worst things that come to us and weaves them in such a way that they actually bring good into our lives. (No wonder I've read that book so many times!)

Elimelech made a terrible decision when he bolted for Moab, and there can be no doubt that it brought "bad" to his family. Even so, the invisible hand of God was working through it all to engineer at least six good results from Elimelech's screw-up in Area 51:

- It brought Naomi back to Bethlehem.
- It brought Naomi back to the Lord.
- It gave widowed and childless Naomi a new family.
- It brought Ruth to the Lord.
- It brought Ruth to Boaz.
- It brought a godly legacy that they never could have imagined.

It's a mystery to our small minds how God is able to do this, but He not only brings good out of bad, He does so with exquisite timing!

John Flavel wrote that "we find a multitude of providences so timed to a minute, that had they occurred just a little sooner or a little later, they had mattered little in comparison with what now they do. Certainly, it cannot be chance, but counsel, that so exactly works in time."[3]

Jeremiah 10:23 states it clearly:

> I know, O LORD, that the way of man is not in himself, that
> it is not in man who walks to direct his steps.

Proverbs 16:9 (NASB) clarifies this teaching with the words "The mind of man plans his way, but the LORD directs his steps."

Did Elimelech plan on his own to turn from God and run to the godless nation of Moab? Yes, he did. Was he, and he alone, responsible for his choice? Yes, he was. And through that entire time, was the Lord governing his will and directing his steps?

Yes.

Where was his wife, Naomi, in this decision? "Did he make the decision himself, or in consultation with Naomi? Or did she perhaps even drive him to it?"[4] Was Naomi responsible for her part? Of course she was. And once again the Lord was overseeing with His invisible hand the free decision-making process of both husband and wife.

This is what Joseph had in mind when he said to his brothers in Genesis 50:20, "As for you, you meant evil against me, but God meant it for good, to bring it about that many people should be kept alive, as they are today."

J. I. Packer explained it like this: "Though all human acts are free in the sense of being self-determined, none are free from God's control according to his eternal purpose and foreordination."

Doesn't that make the Lord responsible for the evil that occurs?

No. It is impossible for the Lord to be responsible for evil. Psalm 145:17 (KJV) states that "The LORD is righteous in all his ways, and holy in all his works."

Note that He is righteous in *all* His ways and works—not some. Thomas Boston hit the nail on the head:

> God is neither the physical nor moral cause of the evil of any action, more than he who rides on a lame horse is the cause of his halting. All the evil that is in sinful actions proceeds and flows from the wicked agent, as the stench of the dunghill does not proceed from the heat of the sun, but from the corrupt matter contained in the dunghill.[5]

Elimelech was responsible for his sin, and we are responsible for our sin. And so God continues to weave His providential tapestry in our lives, interweaving both the bad and the good, and causing good to triumph for those who love Him (Rom. 8:28)—which results in His people giving great glory to His name.

A tapestry is a heavy fabric with a woven pattern or picture, used as a wall hanging. If you've ever seen a tapestry, you know one side comprises a captivating picture or scene, perhaps from a historic battle. Turn it over, however, and all you see is chaos—an incomprehensible jumble of knots and threads.

Oftentimes we look at the events of our lives and all we see is chaos—no beauty, no wonderful image that brings peace to the soul—just absolute pain that seems to have no meaning. But if we could see the other side of the tapestry, we would see the beautiful, providential work that God is weaving together to make sense and beauty out of our lives.

Edith Schaeffer described the work of her and husband, Francis, in the aptly titled book *The Tapestry*. In so doing, she captured the great sense of God's providential working in history.

> You are a thread, and I am a thread. As we affect each other's ideas, physical beings, spiritual understanding, or material possessions, or as we influence each other's attitudes—creativity, courage, determination to keep on, moods, priorities, understanding, spiritually, intellectually, emotionally—we are at the same time affecting history. History is different because you have lived, and because I have lived. We have each caused ripples that will never end, and we continue to cause ripples.
>
> "God has no chance behind Him" is a statement my husband often makes. Of course we are to realize God has a plan. The Bible frequently tells us of the fact that God will guide us, not just temporarily in a tough spot, but "to the end." God is our "counselor," "guide," as well as "father" and "friend." As we look back at what we can see of The Tapestry behind us, we thrill over some of the wonder of how God has woven people together, woven their lives together, woven their talents together, and how He has brought them into contact to be woven side by side in a pattern that has continuity with other parts of the pattern!
>
> The Tapestry speaks immediately of a Designer, an Artist, a Weaver, and of threads being held in his or her hands. We know very well from Adam and Eve and the Fall, that their individual choice brought about the abnormal

events that are still happening as a result. Their effect on history was pretty devastating. So the threads need to ask The Designer, The Weaver, The Artist, time after time to be used in the pattern where He would have them to be. It is not automatic. Mystery? Yes, a mystery that is without solution for the finite mind but completely understood by our Infinite God.[6]

Romans 8:28 contains a great truth, one of the greatest that God has given to us. *How* it works remains a mystery, but maybe it's enough for us to simply know in our heart of hearts that it does work, and that it is true:

> And we know that for those who love God all things work together for good, for those who are called according to his purpose.

For those who love Him, God makes all things work together for good—even the horrific plans of Elimelech. Even my stupid plans of the past, and yours as well.

Frankly, that's about the only way we can go on, after we've behaved foolishly, leaped to wrong choices, or generally made a mess of things. We trust God to take the bad, the evil, and the stubbornness of our own hearts, which was sin against Him and pain to others, and turn it to good. We don't know how He will do it and we don't know when. We just hold up His promise and live off it. Instead of dwelling on our past and our failures, we look to Jesus—we fix our eyes on Him—and His promise to bring good out of tragic circumstances that resulted when we went our own way.

Let's do a quick run-through of six "good" things that God brought out of Elimelech's bad. And if the Lord brought good out of Elimelech's "bad," couldn't He do the same for you and me? Of course He can and will, but remember, it's only through resurrection power that it happens.

Six "Bads" Turned to "Goods"

1. Naomi was brought back to Bethlehem.

When life was at its lowest and Naomi had lost all the men in her life, she finally heard a little good news (Ruth 1:5–6). The famine was over in Bethlehem. And just that quickly, something turned in Naomi's heart. *She wanted to go home.* She wanted to put Moab behind her and return to Bethlehem, the "house of bread."

It was time to go home and be with people of God. All of her dreams had died in the ten-year chapter in Moab. It was time to get her feet back on the soil of the Promised Land. Bethlehem was her town and Israel was her nation.

As Jonah ran away from God's assignment, so Naomi—with Elimelech— ran from her assigned post. Interesting isn't it, that both Jonah and Naomi had to hit bottom before they made their way to their God-given place? It's always good to return to the place where God has called us to be.

At a men's conference, I asked for a show of hands to the question "How many of you men had to hit absolute rock bottom before you turned to the Lord?" My eyeball estimate told me somewhere around 60 percent of the men raised their hands. Yes, hitting rock bottom was bad—probably bruising, maybe even crushing. But it enabled them to find the "good" that God intended for them all along.

2. Naomi was brought back to the Lord.

When Naomi went back to Bethlehem, she admitted that she was a bitter woman over the crushing circumstances of her stay in Moab:

> So the two of them went on until they came to Bethlehem.
> And when they came to Bethlehem, the whole town was
> stirred because of them. And the women said, "Is this
> Naomi?" She said to them, "Do not call me Naomi; call me
> Mara, for the Almighty has dealt very bitterly with me. I

went away full, and the LORD has brought me back empty. Why call me Naomi, when the LORD has testified against me and the Almighty has brought calamity upon me?"

So Naomi returned, and Ruth the Moabite her daughter-in-law with her, who returned from the country of Moab. And they came to Bethlehem at the beginning of barley harvest. (Ruth 1:19–22)

Naomi was bitter because when she left ten years prior, her life was full. She had a husband, two sons, and financial provision to make the trip to Moab and get established for their short-term strategic plan. But when the short term turned into a ten-year tragedy, the bitterness was hard to swallow.

Job suffered for being a righteous man, and his wife suffered along with him. Elimelech, an ungodly man, suffered too, and Naomi was right there with him. When Elimelech finally passed away, the disappointment just kept rolling in on that little family. But all the while, the Lord was using the disappointment to drive Naomi back to the Lord and back to Bethlehem where she belonged. That's how the river of providence works.

Jonathan Edwards observed:

> God's providence may not unfitly be compared to a large and long river, having innumerable branches beginning in different regions, and at a great distance one from another, and all conspiring to one common issue. After their very diverse and contrary courses which they hold for a while, yet all gathering more and more together the nearer they come to their common end, and all at length discharging themselves at one mouth into the same ocean.[7]

Naomi found herself in a hopeless situation. Had she supported Elimelech in his decision to leave Bethlehem in the first place, or did she go with him in reluctance? We don't know, but we do know that the grace and mercy of God were getting her out of the land of idols and back to the land of the Living God. And that's the direction we all should be going, no matter where we are today.

Get back to Him!

3. Naomi gained a new family.

Naomi had lost her husband and her two sons. All she had left were two daughters-in-law whom she urged to go back to their family homes in Moab. Neither daughter-in-law had children. So it was just the three women in crisis. Orpah (whose name means "stubborn") went back to her family and their godless idols. But Ruth refused to go back to her family and their wicked land. And God was about to do something remarkable through Ruth that would give Naomi what she never could have imagined.

Isn't that just like the Lord?

4. Ruth came to know the Lord.

In other words, the young woman from Moab was converted and placed her faith in the God of Israel. It's hard to see how that would have ever happened if Elimelech hadn't turned his back on Bethlehem and moved his family to Moab. But he did walk away—which was certainly wrong—and God turned it for good by bringing Ruth to know the one true God.

Notice the contrast between the two daughters-in-law. Of Orpah it was said that she had gone back to her people "and to her gods" (Ruth 1:15). In the next three verses we read how Ruth's heart was completely opposite of Orpah's:

> But Ruth said, "Do not urge me to leave you or to return
> from following you. For where you go I will go, and where
> you lodge I will lodge. Your people shall be my people, and
> your God my God. Where you die I will die, and there will

I be buried. May the Lᴏʀᴅ do so to me and more also if anything but death parts me from you." And when Naomi saw that she was determined to go with her, she said no more.

This is where Ruth was converted. She left her pagan family, her pagan land, and her pagan gods, and willingly embraced the one true God of Naomi. It's obvious there was a deep-seated desire within her to go to Bethlehem, the people and land of Naomi. First Thessalonians 1:9 describes what happened to Ruth as well as the Thessalonians: "*You turned to God from idols to serve the living and true God.*"

5. God brought Ruth to Boaz.

And who doesn't love a love story?

6. God gave a holy legacy to Ruth and Boaz.

Jeff and Cheryl Scruggs are dear friends who have a remarkable ministry to married couples who find their marriages on the rocks. They are being used by the Lord to help these couples rebuild their marriages on the rock of Jesus Christ.

Jeff and Cheryl "get" these couples because their own marriage was once broken—and it seemed like it was beyond repair. They tell their story in their book *I Do Again*.

An attractive young couple, Jeff and Cheryl Scruggs seemed to have it all: professional success, adorable twin daughters, and a good marriage. But their picture-perfect image concealed a widening chasm between two people unable to connect on an intimate, soul-deep level.

After years of frustration, Cheryl's longing for emotional fulfillment led to an affair and, finally, a divorce that left Jeff utterly devastated and seething with anger. Yet, incredibly, seven years later, Jeff and Cheryl once again stood at the altar, promising to "love, honor, and cherish" one another. A new and vibrant love had risen out of the ashes of this family's pain.[8]

And now, the Lord is using them to restore the marriages of others who are just about out of hope.

It's just another example of God bringing good out of the bad of our lives.

That's a home-run, modern-day Boaz-Ruth testimony, isn't it?

God brought good out of the bad—and the result is that the Scruggs family is serving the Lord and impacting people around the world.

But what about the guy who is reading this and the good hasn't happened yet?

Years ago after speaking at a men's conference, I was talking to a few guys who had questions. There was an informal line of sorts, with men waiting to speak to me, and it took me about twenty minutes to talk with each one. But one guy stood back away from the others, waiting for everyone else to finish.

We shook hands, and he told me his name was Joe Elimelech.

(Actually, that's not true—but I'll bet it got your attention.)

I don't remember his name and I don't remember the city we were in—but what I do remember was his anguish. It took just few minutes to explain. Ten or so years before, this guy who was a Christian husband and father got emotionally involved with a woman from his church. Then they got sexually involved, and he divorced his wife, left his kids, and married this other woman—who divorced her husband and got custody of her kids.

At some point, the Lord severely disciplined this man over his sin, and he turned back to the Lord in repentance. He had made a stupid and impulsive plan to take this new woman and go to Area 51, and in so doing had destroyed two families.

The hound of heaven had hunted him down, and now he was a broken man deep in the depths of despair over his sin. He reminded me of the psalmist is Psalm 130. This guy was calling out to the Lord from the depths of his despair.

It would have been a mercy if he could have died like Elimelech. But he was still in town and saw his former wife and her new husband on an occasional basis. His kids were still in high school and he would see them often. And the great pain of his life was that he knew his former wife had married a Christian man—but truly wasn't happy. She was still grieving the loss of what they had before he ran off to Area 51. She had never said that to him, and never did anything that could be interpreted as disloyal to her new husband. But this guy still could read her like a book, and he still could read between the lines of comments that his kids would make.

To further complicate everything, he and his new wife seemed to be misfits from day one. In truth, in his heart of hearts, he regretted ever leaving his first wife. But he knew he could never go back and undo the wrong. He had not only broken the eggs, but now they were scrambled.

So what could he do?

Knowing that I would have only a few minutes with this man, I made one simple suggestion to him. I turned in my Bible and showed him Romans 8:28. I suggested that he memorize the passage and pray it every time he began to despair over the scrambled eggs of his life. For the times when he would think of his kids, I encouraged him to stay connected as best he could and pray Romans 8:28 over them. For the times when he would think of his former wife and her husband, I said that he should immediately pray Romans 8:28 over them and their marriage—and that he should do the same for himself and his new wife.

If you have broken the eggs of your life and/or others', pray Romans 8:28 over each situation and individual. Thank the Lord that only He has the power to unscramble the eggs—or to make an omelet so exquisite that it will be a wonder to everyone.

Don't try to figure out when He will do it or how He will do it.

Simply trust and obey, for there's no other way to be happy in Jesus.

He's still in the business of bringing good out of bad—and it's your business to trust Him to do it.

> **A Boaz Man remembers that God brings very good things out of very bad things.**

CHAPTER SEVEN

HARD STRETCH OF HIGHWAY

"The assured Christian is more motion than notion, more work than word, more life than lip, more hand than tongue."
—Thomas Brooks

In January of 1984, Joseph Schexnider simply dropped off the face of the earth. Just twenty-two years old, he had been scheduled to show up at court to face charges of stealing a car. But he never showed. Not for months, not for years, not for decades.

Now of course, it's not all that unusual for someone to skip out on a court hearing. Eventually they'll either show up or get tracked down.

But not Joseph. He flat out disappeared. It's not so easy to disappear in a small town, but he managed to pull it off. Nobody in Abbeville, Louisiana, had a clue where he was … until May of 2011.[1]

Workers were doing some renovations in a bank in downtown Abbeville that required them to explore an old chimney. The chimney hadn't been used in years and went from the roof to the second floor, and for years the bank had used the second floor only for storage. The small vent leading to the chimney was closed tight and had been ignored for decades. But when they opened it up, they found a skeleton.

Yep, it was Joseph.

He had gotten stuck halfway down that chimney and couldn't move, neither up nor down, and no one could hear his cries for help. The bank conducted all of its business on the first floor. Young Joseph Schexnider experienced a slow and terrible death, and he died all alone.

Why had he crawled into that chimney? To hide? To attempt a bank robbery? No one knows for sure, and Joseph isn't available for interviews. The point is, he made a decision that was unwise and off point.

And it cost him … everything.

Joseph had apparently been in some trouble before and had employed the very same technique. When trouble threatened, he went on the dodge, hiding out until things cooled down. At least once, he joined a traveling circus. But he had always come back. Though young in years, Joseph had experienced his share of troubles and hard times and had obviously taken some wrong turns on the road of life. But crawling down into that narrow chimney was the worst move he ever made.

It was also the last.

We learned from Elimelech that you can't scheme your way through the tight places of life. Eventually, our schemes and dreams will hit a brick wall—or in some cases, a brick chimney.

Here's some good news. When the Lord Jesus Christ comes into our lives, we get a new beginning, and we don't have to run or hide anymore.

It was Alexander Whyte who said that the Christian life is a series of new beginnings. Ruth and Naomi were about to get a new beginning, not just because of where they were headed, but because of whom they would meet when they got there.

His name was Boaz, and as we've noted, his very name means strength.

Boaz was a wise man who was on point and on the job. You wouldn't find men like Boaz hiding out in Moab, sneaking into Area 51, or getting stuck in chimneys. Boaz was the sort of steady, faithful, clear-eyed man whom God uses … and it's the kind of man He wants us to become.

It all began, of course, with Naomi's decision to leave Moab in the rear-view mirror, returning to Bethlehem and ultimately to the Lord.

In chapter 1, Naomi and Ruth were in despair and despondency. But in chapter 2, everything was about to change for these two women.

So what happened? Boaz happened!

Boaz finally showed up in chapter 2, and to quote John Phillips, when he did, he dominated the book! God used this great-grandfather of King David to change everything. Boaz shone out from these early pages of the Old Testament as a model of the Lord Jesus Christ, who rescues us, cares for us, protects us, and sustains us. The Lord Jesus turns our lives around, giving us a new heart and a new perspective.

When Christ comes into our lives, it changes the way we look at life. Instead of being afraid of death, we begin to understand that death is simply a promotion into heaven. Remember how Jesus expressed it to His grieving friend Martha?

"Whoever believes in me, though he die, yet shall he live, and everyone who lives and believes in me shall never die" (John 11:25–26).

And by the way, if you imagine heaven to be lounging on a cloud in a wispy white robes strumming on a harp—or sitting on a hard pew through an eternal church service—forget that nonsense. Do you think that's all God has planned for you for eternity? Well, think again.

Heaven is our ultimate destination, not life on this earth.

Before we come to know Christ, we find ourselves caught up with grabbing everything we can on this earth. Scripture, however, teaches us that this isn't home at all. We're travelers, just passing through. Going through life on earth is like walking through an airport, pulling your black suitcase on wheels. Your real destination isn't some gate at a crowded airport; that's just the launch point.

We're on a journey, and those who occupy God's Hall of Fame in Hebrews 11 knew that very well.

> It was by faith that Abraham obeyed when God called him to leave home and go to another land that God would give him as his inheritance. He went without knowing where he was going. And even when he reached the land God promised him, he lived there by faith—for he was like a foreigner, living in tents. And so did Isaac and Jacob, who inherited the same promise. Abraham was confidently looking forward to a city with eternal foundations, a city designed and built by God. (vv. 8–10 NLT)

Abraham was on a lifetime voyage, and he knew very well the trip wouldn't be over until he died. Only then would he find his home in the eternal city.

We are on a journey—a sometimes difficult and heartbreaking journey—and there are certain principles that give us hope when life begins to feel unbearable. The providence of God leads us through all of our years, from womb to tomb. Even before you knew God, He was leading you. His providence leads us *to* Christ and then leads us *with* Christ as our Shepherd.

But make no mistake: it isn't always a pleasure trip. Just as there are incredible vistas and scenic stretches of parkway along this road trip called life, there are also some rough, rugged, dangerous canyons, deserts, and mountain passes that have to be crossed as well.

Some people, however, try to maintain an illusion of heaven on earth.

I read the story of a man who has attempted to make his life journey as easy and uneventful as possible—and apparently has enough money to pull it off. Successful in his career, he maintains a lifestyle most people could only dream about, including three homes in three different states.

The article in the *Wall Street Journal* is titled "One Home, Three Locations: An author's nearly identical houses reflect his desire for absolute consistency."[2] Each home has been furnished and decorated almost identically. Leather chairs, tweed curtains, carpet, you name it. Even his office in each home is a replica of the other two. Same wood paneling, same desk, same computer, same monitor and keyboard, same software, same chair, same phone system, same printer in the same location. Probably the same snacks lodged in identical refrigerators.

And did I mention his dogs? He has three of them: yellow labs that all answer to the name "Fred." So far, he has had a total of four yellow labs. When one dies, a new yellow lab is brought in and named—you guessed it—Fred.

This is a man who likes to live his life in 70 degree weather. He doesn't appreciate getting too hot in the summer, nor will he tolerate becoming too cold in the winter. Flying in his own plane, he rotates between his three homes, depending on which home in which climate zone is closest to the 70 degree mark.

The man was quoted as saying, "You get into certain grooves. I have certain requirements." He is a man who, at the age of seventy-three, likes precision and order. Too bad it won't last forever.

Joseph Schexnider got stuck in a chimney in Louisiana. This man has three chimneys, but I would venture to say that he's just as stuck in the wrong place as young Joseph was. One man had a hard journey, and another is enjoying an easy journey—for a season. And then comes the reality of the next life.

Boaz made his first appearance in chapter 2 of the book of Ruth. But before he showed up, Naomi and Ruth had to make a hard and treacherous journey. Just like we're doing right now.

> So the two of them continued on their journey. When they came to Bethlehem, the entire town was excited by their arrival. "Is it really Naomi?" the women asked.
>
> "Don't call me Naomi," she responded. "Instead, call me Mara, for the Almighty has made life very bitter for me. I went away full, but the LORD has brought me home empty. Why call me Naomi when the LORD has caused me to suffer and the Almighty has sent such tragedy upon me?"
>
> So Naomi returned from Moab, accompanied by her daughter-in-law Ruth, the young Moabite woman. They arrived in Bethlehem in late spring, at the beginning of the barley harvest.
>
> Now there was a wealthy and influential man in Bethlehem named Boaz, who was a relative of Naomi's husband, Elimelech. (Ruth 1:19–2:1 NLT)

The return trip from Moab to Bethlehem was only about fifty miles as the crow flies. But these two women weren't crows and they weren't flying:

> The journey from Moab to Bethlehem had to be extremely arduous for the two women. First, they would have traveled north to skirt the Dead Sea. Then, to cross the Jordan, they would have had to descend from a relatively high elevation to 1,290 feet *below* sea level where the Jordan River enters the Dead Sea. After making their way across the river, they would begin their ascent through rugged terrain … to reach

Bethlehem, 2,300 feet above sea level in the hill country of Judah. Not an easy trek.[3]

For the last ten years, it had been a hard journey. But they had to do one last leg in the triathlon to get back to Bethlehem. And the last lap is always the hardest. It wasn't the scenic route; it was the *brutal* route, with countless ups and downs. It was a difficult passage, and for Ruth, at least, a journey into the unknown. Neither of them had any idea at that point that a man named Boaz would be there in Bethlehem—and that everything would change for the better.

What was the significance of Boaz?

Boaz was the only man within a hundred miles who could pull them out of trouble. Any man can pull over and help a stranded woman change a flat tire. But this was major-league trouble Naomi and Ruth were in, and under the requirements of the Old Testament, it took a certain kind of man to rescue them from their dilemma.

The fact is only a qualified "kinsman-redeemer" would do, and less than a handful of men fit the requirements. And even if someone did meet the stringent obligations, it would take a strong and courageous man to step up and take on the responsibilities of caring for two women. Not every man in the clan was willing to make that kind of sacrifice.

Boaz was the man who would do that for Ruth, and the Lord Jesus Christ is the One who sacrificially stepped in and saved us out of sin and death.

> The concept of the Kinsman-Redeemer or *goel* (3:9, close relative) is an important portrayal of the work of Christ. The *goel* must (1) be related by blood to those he redeems (see Deuteronomy 25:5, 7-10; John 1:14); (2) be able to pay the price of redemption (see 2:1; 1 Peter 1:18-19); (3) be willing to redeem (see 3:11; Matthew 20:28; John 10:15); and (4) be free himself (Christ was free from the curse of sin).

The *goel*, used thirteen times in this short book (of Ruth),
presents a clear picture of the mediating work of Christ.[4]

In Ephesians 2:8, we find the familiar phrase "For by grace you have
been saved through faith." The Lord Jesus is the great Boaz, the great Savior,
who went to the cross and took our sin upon Himself. Martin Luther said,
"Jesus was the greatest sinner." How can that be, since Jesus lived a sinless life?
Luther simply meant that when Jesus took upon Himself my sin, your sin, and
the sins of world, He became the greatest sinner. Although He had no sin of
His own, He took our sin and died in our place, paying the penalty due to us
with His own blood.

That's what makes the Lord Jesus the ultimate Kinsman-Redeemer. But
note this: He doesn't just save us once. We read, "For by grace you have been
saved." The construction of that phrase in the original text indicates that *we
have been saved with continuing results.*[5]

In other words, He saves us when we come to Him, and He *keeps saving
us* as we travel the hard trail through this life. He has saved us with continuing
results, and that means He just keeps on saving us from sin, from ourselves, and
from dumb decisions. He continues to be faithful when we need to be saved.
He wasn't just our Savior once upon a time; He is our Savior through every day
of life.

He loves us and wants us to grow and mature, so He will discipline us when
we need it and humble us often; but it's all part of the continuing results of
being saved by grace. The grace keeps coming as we travel through life. If you're
on a hard stretch of trail right now, that news ought to encourage your heart.
You're not in this by yourself. Not ever.

I see three lessons arising from the hard journey that took the two women
from Moab and back to Bethlehem—and ultimately to the encounter with
Boaz. I think these three lessons are true for every Christian as we travel through
this life. We're like the men who bought Conestoga wagons, filled them with
necessary provisions—flour, sugar, salt, skillet, Dutch oven, medicinal whiskey,

rifles, Colts, and ammunition—put their wives and kids on board, tied their milk cows to the back, and headed west for Oregon or California. Their ultimate dream? To homestead 160 acres and carve out a new life on the American frontier.

We too are travelers, moving through the days and years of our lives. But our true destination has never been an earthly homestead. That comes when we die or when the Lord returns. Our homestead isn't 160 acres—it's the new earth and the New Jerusalem. Until then, we are traveling men who live each day trusting in the faithfulness of God to fulfill His promises to us at the exact moment they are needed (Heb. 11:1–6).

Those men in the Conestoga wagons didn't turn on their satellite radios to get a report from the traffic helicopters circling overhead as to why traffic was backing up through the pass. And they didn't call AAA roadside assistance on their cell phones when they broke an axle. It was a hard, relentless, and exhausting journey traveling across a whole continent as they did, and there were undoubtedly days when they thought they couldn't go on.

That happens to us even with all of our technology, GPS, Wi-Fi, and tweets. We've got more information than we know what we to do with. But what we are lacking isn't information; it's perspective.

When life gets brutally hard on the trail and you don't see how you can possibly handle the stress and strain for another minute, you have to get yourself under control and get perspective. Sometimes all you can see from your vantage point are high walls and towering obstacles. And you wonder how in the world you will navigate the financial, relational, or health roadblock that threatens your very existence.

But this is where you have to take a step back and get a wider view. You have to mentally get into the traffic helicopter that is hovering two or three thousand feet overhead. And when you do that, you can look down the road and see what's ahead. You can see your way through the pass and see that in just another couple of miles, you'll be out of the desert and about to find a bubbling artesian spring surrounded by beautiful trees and sweet green grass to graze your animals.

In the day-to-day grind of a hard highway, you can gain that level of perspective only by putting God's Word into your heart and mind. You can't see down the road ten miles because you're in rush-hour traffic, just trying to get home for dinner. So how do you change your perspective on the immediate and pressing circumstances of everyday life (especially when you find yourself becoming worn down, frustrated, and fatigued)?

You have to remember that God sees the entire journey. He created you, placed you on earth, brought you to Christ, and oversees every day and every event of your life, until He gets you to your homestead in heaven. Jesus didn't say that there are homesteads in heaven, but in John 14:2 (KJV) He did say that He would have a mansion waiting for us upon our arrival. (I'd settle for a log cabin with a 360-degree view.)

The only thing that keeps us sane on the hard trail is the sure knowledge that God is in His heaven, governing the entire universe. Psalm 103:19 (NASB) declares, "The LORD has established His throne in the heavens, and His sovereignty rules over all." In other words, He has absolute control over our world and all its events. Psalm 115:3 (NASB) affirms that "our God is in the heavens; He does whatever He pleases."

Only the sovereignty of God and the providence of God over every detail of the universe and your life can bring peace to your heart on a bitter stretch of trail. Those two truths defeat anxiety whenever they are embraced and believed.

And so we find hope as we make the journey through this life.

Three lessons stand out from the hard stretch of trail from Moab back to Bethlehem.

Lesson 1: God can lead you through a series of defeats and still give you a breakthrough.

It had been ten years of disappointment and difficulty for Naomi, with one setback after another. The man who wrote Psalm 42 hadn't been born yet, but Naomi would have agreed with his sentiments in verse 7

(NASB), where he wrote, "All Your breakers and Your waves have rolled over me."

It feels like that sometimes, doesn't it? Disappointments and afflictions often come in sets. Surfers know that waves come in sets, but oftentimes tourists don't. They will drive by Pacific Coast Highway in California and wonder why all those surfers are just sitting out there on their boards, looking at the horizon. That's because they're waiting for the next set of waves. Waves come in sets, maybe three to ten at a time, followed by an interval of three to five minutes (give or take) until the next set rolls in.

It has been my experience that disappointments and hardships on the road of life often come in sets of threes. I can't give you any stats on that and I wouldn't die for that observation. It's just something I've noticed through personal experience. One affliction comes, knocks you off your feet, you're just managing to get back up, and then BOOM!—here comes another setback that hits you so hard it knocks the wind out of you. You're just starting to breathe again and get your bearings, and then from your blindside WHAM-O! Yet another wave of affliction comes in, smashing over your head, and it's all you can do to figure out which way is up so you can get to the surface and breathe.

In Job 1:13–19, Job got hit with four waves—four killer tsunamis stacked one on top of another:

> Now there was a day when his sons and daughters were eating and drinking wine in their oldest brother's house, and there came a messenger to Job and said, "The oxen were plowing and the donkeys feeding beside them, and the Sabeans fell upon them and took them and struck down the servants with the edge of the sword, and I alone have escaped to tell you." While he was yet speaking, there came another and said, "The fire of God fell from heaven and burned up the sheep and the servants and consumed them, and I alone have

escaped to tell you." While he was yet speaking, there came another and said, "The Chaldeans formed three groups and made a raid on the camels and took them and struck down the servants with the edge of the sword, and I alone have escaped to tell you." While he was yet speaking, there came another and said, "Your sons and daughters were eating and drinking wine in their oldest brother's house, and behold, a great wind came across the wilderness and struck the four corners of the house, and it fell upon the young people, and they are dead, and I alone have escaped to tell you."

Stuff happens, to godly people, to Christians.

In the Christian life, waves of hardship are not abnormal; they are normal. Peter told a group of persecuted believers, "Beloved, do not be surprised at the fiery trial when it comes upon you to test you, as though something strange were happening to you" (1 Peter 4:12). In fact, it isn't "strange" at all. It's only to be expected. Paul stated flatly, "Through many tribulations we must enter the kingdom of God" (Acts 14:22).

But here's the good news. Those hardships are for our testing to see if we're teachable, and willing to submit and learn the lessons. And disappointing and difficult as those hard times might be, they won't last forever. "Many are the afflictions of the righteous, but the LORD delivers him out of them all" (Ps. 34:19).

He brought Job out of his affliction, and He can bring you out as well.

Is anything—I mean *anything*—too hard for the Lord? You know the answer to that question. Nothing is too hard for Him. That's why He can tie together a series of insurmountable setbacks and give you a breakthrough—at the very moment when you think that you're finished.

Sometimes our hardships don't hit like a series of waves but rather like one terrible, prolonged storm. Did you see the movie *The Perfect Storm*? Psalm 107:23–30 describes life when a perfect storm hits:

Some went down to the sea in ships,

> doing business on the great waters;

they saw the deeds of the LORD,

> his wondrous works in the deep.

For he commanded and raised the stormy wind,

> which lifted up the waves of the sea.

They mounted up to heaven; they went down to the depths;

> their courage melted away in their evil plight;

they reeled and staggered like drunken men

> and were at their wits' end.

Then they cried to the LORD in their trouble,

> and he delivered them from their distress.

He made the storm be still,

> and the waves of the sea were hushed.

Then they were glad that the waters were quiet,

> and he brought them to their desired haven.

Did you catch the last verse? It's dripping with understatement. *"They were glad that the waters were quiet."* I guess so! Finally, after days of countless gut-churning, vomit-inducing, Empire State Building–size waves, it all went quiet and God brought them to their desired haven. And, oh man, were they glad.

As that psalmist knew so well, God is able to sustain you through a series of insurmountable setbacks and give you a breakthrough where you had never imagined one to be. As John Flavel said, "He has either strengthened your back to bear, or lightened your burden, or else opened an unexpected door of escape according to His promise (1 Corinthians 10:13), so that the evil which you feared did not come upon you."[6]

Lesson 2: Hard journeys often lead to surprising outcomes.

If you would, get this picture in your mind one more time. Ruth and Naomi were making the hard trek back to Bethlehem, and they didn't have a clue what God had planned for them when they showed up. They were simply trying to survive and fight off starvation. But the Lord had so much more in mind for them than bare existence!

Journeying as they were through the pit of the earth—a perfect description of trekking around the Dead Sea—their spirits had to be brutally low. What a terrible passage for two women through a hostile, forsaken wilderness. There would have been no water to drink, other than what they could carry. They might have been able to wade through the edges of the Dead Sea to cool their exhausted feet, but there was no drinking it! The water there has the highest salt content of any body of water on the face of the earth. There are so many minerals in that water that it will float a three-hundred-pound man. But it's not Perrier spring water, and that's what they needed.

Life was bitter on the trail, and the future wasn't looking any better.

That's how it was back in the autumn of 1849 for a young woman named Janette Riker. In what would later be known as Montana, Janette, "her father, and two brothers, stopped their wagon for a few days to hunt buffalo before continuing over the mountains to Oregon. The men left camp early on the second day and never returned."[7]

Not only did they never return, but they were also never heard from again—and they certainly weren't lodged in a brick chimney somewhere. Grizzly bears, however, roamed that region, and Indian war parties were constantly on the move. So only God knows what happened to the Riker men.

One thing is for sure: they had been a close family, and they would have never abandoned a teenage girl in the wilderness. Nevertheless, that's what happened. They had camped in a beautiful little valley in the mountains for a few days, and there were no towns or settlements for miles and miles. At some point Janette finally must have admitted to herself that something awful had happened, and her men would not be coming back.

Winter was coming. Montana winters and blizzards are legendary, and in that little valley she would become snowed in. And that's precisely what happened. She made do with the best preparations she knew how to make, but when the Indians found her some five months later, she barely had a pulse.

The Indians were so impressed with her courage that they took the starving young woman with them and got her to the fort at Walla Walla.[8] Against all odds, Janette survived, regained her health, married a rancher, and raised a family. She had endured many days in chest-high snow when she thought her trail had played out. What she couldn't have known, however, was that many days of blessing and favor awaited in her future. She simply had no idea of what was to come.

Are you familiar with Jeremiah 29:11? It's an oft quoted verse: "For I know the plans I have for you, declares the LORD, plans for welfare and not for evil, to give you a future and a hope."

What is not so well-known is that it was written by Jeremiah to a group of Hebrew exiles who had been hauled off to Babylon. They were on the worst stretch of trail they could have ever imagined. It wasn't where they wanted to be. But the Lord had an outcome for them, a great and surprising outcome already taken care of and arranged. He simply had it waiting in the wings, and He would bring it out at the right time.

It was true for the exiles, it was true for Ruth and Naomi as they scrambled over those Judean rocks in the wilderness, and it's true for you and me. He's got something in mind. C. S. Lewis referred to his experience as being surprised by joy. Are you on the long, brutal road as you read this? Stay the course—and feed on His faithfulness.

Lesson 3: Great blessing is often preceded by a hard stretch of highway.

The hardest stretch of trail I've ever been on was the two-year stretch of depression that hit me in my early thirties. It got so bad that I had days when I truly wished I could die. For two straight years, I had no joy. I'm not proud of that, but it's the truth. I wasn't trying to make it through the day—I was trying to make it to lunch without falling apart.

What I didn't know was that God was getting me ready for a surprising outcome and a time of lasting productivity and joy. I've lived long enough now to understand that the best of times are often preceded by the worst of times. God takes us down the brutal trail to prepare our hearts so we can handle greater favor in the future. But great darkness and depression often threaten us before the days of favor show up.

C. H. Spurgeon described it well:

> This depression comes over me whenever the Lord is pre-
> paring a greater blessing for my ministry; the cloud is black
> before it breaks, and overshadows before it yields its deluge
> of mercy. Depression has now become to me as a prophet
> in rough clothing, a John the Baptist, heralding the nearer
> coming of my Lord's richer [blessing]. So have far better
> men found it. The scouring of the vessel has fitted it for
> the Master's use.... The Lord is revealed in the backside of
> the desert, while His servant keeps the sheep and waits in
> solitary awe. The wilderness is the way to Canaan. The low
> valley is the way to the towering mountain. Defeat prepares
> for victory.[9]

In other words, stay the course.

Boaz is just around the corner.

A Boaz Man looks for the breakthrough in every setback.

CHAPTER EIGHT

BOAZ RIDES IN

"A godly man prefers grace before goods, and wisdom before the world."
—Richard Bernard

The chapter title above isn't really accurate, but I liked the sound of it. So there it is.

The truth is Boaz never had to ride *in*, because he never rode *out*. We don't have any local news footage or surveillance video of him galloping into Bethlehem, because he never left. He stayed in town for the whole ten years covered in the first chapter of the book of Ruth.

Boaz fulfilled 1 Corinthians 4:2 some thirteen hundred years before Paul ever penned it on a scroll.

"It is required of stewards that they be found faithful" (KJV).

Boaz was faithful in Bethlehem before the famine, he was faithful during the famine, and he was faithful when the famine finally passed by and the leading economic indicators began picking up speed again.

In other words, Boaz was *reliable*.

Here's another good word: he was *dependable*.

He was the kind of man who could be counted on to get the job done. He didn't whine, didn't see himself as a victim, and didn't call in sick when he wasn't.

We had a medium-size Texas hailstorm roll through the area. That means ping-pong-ball-size hail. The accompanying wind took down our two big canopied oak trees, and the hail roughed up everything else. We were fortunate, because all the windows in our house didn't shatter. But that's exactly what happened to hundreds of homes just a couple of miles from here.

What's a *big*-size Texas hailstorm? In the same storm, just a hundred miles from here, people were getting softball-size hail. And that stuff can kill you. The insurance adjuster who wrote my estimate had just come from the softball side of the storm and let me know how fortunate I was to just get the ping-pong variety.

Even so, the hail and wind damaged our roof, and the roofers have been here for the last couple of days. I've got to hand it to them … these guys showed up right on time and worked all day until dark. The next day, they did it all over again, finishing up just after sunset. It's August as I write these words, and the temperature has been right around 110. Up on the roof it had to be 125 to 130.

I told those guys they were real men, and I meant it.

They committed to do a job, showed up in record-breaking heat, and didn't call their mommies to take them home. They started early, worked hard, stayed hydrated, and finished late. I'd recommend this crew to anyone. Why? Because they were reliable, dependable, and faithful.

Those are Boaz traits.

When Ruth and Naomi walked into town, Boaz was already there, because that was his assigned post. Where else would he be?

We've already made the point that Boaz is an Old Testament picture of the Lord Jesus Christ. The Lord Jesus is the ultimate Boaz—the ultimate Kinsman-Redeemer.

To get a full comparison, then, let's take a minute and look at the first thirty years that Jesus spent on the earth.

"Is Not This the Carpenter?"

Wait a minute, you're saying. We can't look at the Lord's first thirty years, because we don't have any information about that time. Yes, we know He was born of a virgin in Bethlehem, taken as an infant to Egypt to flee Herod, and then ended up in Nazareth after Herod died (Matt. 1–2). Jesus was sometimes called "the Nazarene" because Nazareth was the town where He was raised.

But what else do we know?

When Jesus was twelve, the little family went down to Jerusalem for the Passover, and on the way back home, they couldn't locate Him among the relatives. Eventually, they went back to Jerusalem and found Him in the temple, interacting with the teachers of the Law (Luke 2:39–52). Everyone was amazed at this wisdom and sorry to see Him go back to Nazareth with His parents.

And that's all we know about the first thirty years of His life.

Except for one other fact.

We know that He was a carpenter.

> He went away from there and came to his hometown, and his disciples followed him. And on the Sabbath he began to teach in the synagogue, and many who heard him were aston-ished, saying, "Where did this man get these things? What is

the wisdom given to him? How are such mighty works done by his hands? Is not this the carpenter, the son of Mary and brother of James and Joses and Judas and Simon? And are not his sisters here with us?" And they took offense at him. And Jesus said to them, "A prophet is not without honor, except in his hometown and among his relatives and in his own household." And he could do no mighty work there, except that he laid his hands on a few sick people and healed them. And he marveled because of their unbelief. (Mark 6:1–6)

This account is from the time that Jesus, having launched His public ministry at the age of thirty, returned to His hometown of Nazareth and was rejected. Much has been written on this event, but I simply want to point out that when He returned, they referred to Him as "the carpenter."

This gives us a major hint as to what He was doing since the time He was twelve and in the temple.

- Jesus lived in the same community.
- Jesus lived in obscurity.
- Jesus was part of a family.
- Jesus knew poverty and hard times.
- Jesus worked at His trade.

You could say much the same about Boaz on that day when Ruth and Naomi showed up in Bethlehem. And you might be able to say those same things about yourself and your daily existence as well.

Not long ago, my son Josh put me on to an old, out-of-print book from the 1800s titled *The Life of Lives* by F. W. Farrar. While I like the man's name, I don't agree with all of his theological conclusions. Be that as it may, Josh told me about a particular chapter in this book, "The Lessons of the Unrecorded Years," and its remarkable observations.

In the workshop at Nazareth, faithful in that which was little, Christ revealed to man where to seek and how to enjoy the true riches.... His was a life of manual (labor) and toil.... There has been a haughty tendency in all ages to despise manual labour, and look down on those who live by it.... What sublimer lesson could Jesus have taught to mankind than by spending thirty unknown years as the humble Carpenter of Nazareth? ... The object of life—as the silent, unrecorded years of Christ's life teach us—is neither to be known, nor to be praised, but simply to do our duty and to the best of our power to serve our brother-men.... By living this unknown life as a peasant in a Galilean village, Christ set the very example, and taught the very lesson, which the untold millions most deeply need.[1]

Os Guinness took the principle to its biblical conclusion:

We are not primarily called to do something or go somewhere; *we are called to Someone.* We are not called first to special work but to God. The key to answering the call is to be devoted to no one and to nothing above God himself. As [Oswald] Chambers said, "The men and women our Lord sends out on His enterprises are the ordinary human stuff, plus dominating devotion to Himself wrought by the Holy Spirit." The most frequent phrase in his writings: "Be absolutely His."[2]

"Absolutely His"

When Jesus lived in obscurity, it was His desire to do the will of the Father and to glorify His Father, as He clearly stated when His life and ministry became public.

You see, that's where faithfulness, reliability, and dependence ultimately come from. It's a desire to "be absolutely His."

Jesus was absolutely committed to the Father in all things. And as children of our heavenly Father, that's our calling too.

That's why Boaz stayed at his post and remained faithful. That's why he served the Lord in mid-life as a single man without a wife or children and why he would later serve the Lord when he was surprised with the gift of a family. Margaret Thatcher once said, "There is no society, only individuals and families."

Notice the providential timing of God as the story begins to unfold. Something wondrous was about to happen in the lives of Ruth and Naomi. They were about to encounter Boaz, a man who was faithful, steadfast, and at his post. These women were in trouble, but they weren't government statistics; they were individuals. What they needed was a family—and a family man who could become their kinsman-redeemer.

Boaz was about to become that for them. And the real secret behind Boaz was that he was "absolutely His." Because of that, Boaz made himself available to be a responsible and sacrificial leader.

Isn't that what we aspire to be as men? What does that look like? We may not be in the public eye or some huge platform of influence, but that doesn't mean that our lives or our assignments are unimportant. We know in our gut that there is nothing more important than functioning as an effective leader at our assigned posts. Boaz functioned in his little world, and I want to function effectively in mine. But how does a man learn to be a good leader if he never saw good leadership during his childhood?

Walk with the Wise

Solomon gave us an insightful—and very hopeful—answer in Proverbs 13:20 (NASB), writing, "He who walks with wise men will be wise."

That's why we're figuratively walking with Boaz through the pages of this book. We're taking the opportunity to see a godly man at work. We're making time to observe a faithful man, who belonged fully to the Lord, handle an unforeseen crisis that could potentially turn into the greatest blessing of his life. In the process, we're going to watch this guy demonstrate the marks of mature male leadership.

If you didn't learn how to be a spiritual leader from your dad, then how would you know what to do? Maybe you find yourself struggling with spiritual leadership in your home because you never saw it as a kid growing up. Maybe your dad couldn't show you how to be a spiritual leader because his dad couldn't show *him*.

You see, this lack of male leadership goes back generations. And as I have said many times, it's time to put a new link in the family chain.

That's why we're going to watch Boaz as he handled this situation with two desperate women. And we will see a model of balanced, masculine, godly leadership.

Randy Stinson and Dan Dumas have written a solid little book titled *A Guide to Biblical Manhood*. It's brief, biblical, and extremely practical. Stinson and Dumas "get" men. They know what makes them tick. And they put the cookies on the lower shelf so that any man, younger or older, can benefit greatly from their insights.

They have come up with nine traits that describe how a godly man actually leads:

> Vision: *This is where we are going.*
> Direction: *This is how we get there.*
> Instruction: *Let me show you how.*
> Imitation: *Watch me.*
> Inspiration: *Isn't this great?*
> Affirmation: *You're doing great.*
> Evaluation: *How are we doing?*

Correction: *Let's make a change.*

Protection and Provision: *I'll take care of you.*

As we helicopter through the next three chapters in the book of Ruth, watch how these nine principles are woven together in the story. It's what godly men do as they get up and face the everyday challenges of life. These nine traits create and maintain a positive atmosphere in a home.

It doesn't mean we're positive and optimistic because life is one pleasant, sunny stroll down Easy Street. No, we know better than that. What it means is that even though life is hard and difficult, a godly man leading a family will bring a sense of security, confidence, and affirmation that keeps the family morale up and not down. When a husband-father makes it clear that the Lord is his Shepherd and that he is trusting in the Lord to give him the wisdom to lead his family, there is an underlying sense of peace and stability in the home. Everybody wins when that is the case.

And now … back to our story.

> So Naomi returned, and Ruth the Moabite her daughter-in-law with her, who returned from the country of Moab. And they came to Bethlehem at the beginning of barley harvest.
>
> Now Naomi had a relative of her husband's, a worthy man of the clan of Elimelech, whose name was Boaz. And Ruth the Moabite said to Naomi, "Let me go to the field and glean among the ears of grain after him in whose sight I shall find favor." And she said to her, "Go, my daughter." So she set out and went and gleaned in the field after the reapers, and she happened to come to the part of the field belonging to Boaz, who was of the clan of Elimelech. (Ruth 1:22–2:3)

There are three truths that demand our close attention here.

- Providence ordained Naomi and Ruth's time
- Providence ordained the right benefit.
- Providence ordained the right field.

Providence Ordained Their Time of Arrival

After their brutal and difficult journey, Ruth and Naomi arrived in Bethlehem at the time of spring harvest. The barley crop was just starting to come in, which would be quickly followed by the wheat harvest.

In the providence of God, they didn't arrive in the winter. God ordained their circumstances and their decision to return to Bethlehem so that their arrival would coincide with the barley harvest. If they had arrived four weeks prior, it would have been too soon, and if they had arrived three months later, the harvest would have been over. They arrived at precisely the right time. The harvest was just beginning and because the timing of God was perfect, they could take advantage of a benefit that God had written into the law of Israel. But this benefit would be available only at times of harvest.

Providence Ordained the Right Benefit

Gleaning the fields behind the harvesters was a benefit God provided for the poor of the land. According to Leviticus 19:9 and Deuteronomy 24:19, a landowner was not to harvest every square inch of his field. He was commanded by the Lord to leave the corners of his field unharvested. Beyond this, he was instructed not to go over his field a second time to gather up what had been missed on the first pass. This was to allow the widows, the orphans, and the poor to work the fields and gather enough so that they might survive and not die of hunger.

This was a benefit that God extended to those in need, and once again, the Lord was looking out for Naomi and Ruth.

It's also important to remember that this was a time in Israel when many in the land were living in outright rebellion to God. It's probable that very few landowners thought to follow God's command to leave the corners for the needy.

Boaz, however, was a man who feared the Lord, walked with Him, and cared very much about God's priorities and commands. He was "all in" with the Lord—his commitment extending even to his crops and to his giving.

Providence Ordained the Right Field

Ruth, of course, knew very little of all this. All she knew was that she had an opportunity to get some groceries by gleaning in the field. She asked Naomi for permission to glean, and Naomi gave her approval. And then the Scriptures tell us, "So she set out and went and gleaned in the field after the reapers, and she happened to come to the part of the field belonging to Boaz, who was of the clan of Elimelech" (Ruth 2:3).

So Ruth headed out to the field, hoping and praying that the Lord would lead her to a field with a good harvest for that day. If you were in her shoes, wouldn't you be praying that prayer as you headed out to the fields? Sure you would. And that's exactly what happened. The Lord directed her steps to the right field among all the fields.

Note the term "she happened." Sinclair Ferguson made this observation:

> This is a somewhat sanitized version of what the author actually wrote. More literally translated, the words are something like this: "the happenstance that happened to her was...." As the theologians put in succinct fashion, events that are certain to God are unpredictable and contingent

from our point of view. There are many things in our lives that seem to "happen" to us by happenstance, things that we may never understand. From Ruth's point of view things do "just happen." She has no idea about the significance of gleaning in Boaz's field. She probably does not even know who Boaz is!

Here then the author is helping us to view our lives as though they were being played out on a split screen on which we see both the sovereignty of God and his lordship over all the details of our lives, and also the contingency or unpredictability of the events of the world in which we live. From a human point of view, everything could be quite different from the way it is.

Yet at the same time we recognize that in the midst of our confusion and happenstances and surprise of life there is a sovereign God in heaven whose hand is upon us every moment of the day, a God who reigns over every inch of the universe in which we lie. So we know that nothing "just happens...."

That is why we can be quietly confident—not because we know exactly what God is doing in this unpredictable world, but because we know that what is unpredictable to us is already predicted by him.[3]

So Ruth, who had never been to Bethlehem before in her life, headed out to the fields and decided to stop and ask permission to glean in a certain field. When she did, she had no idea that the land belonged to Boaz, a blood relative of Elimelech and of her former husband, Mahlon.

She had no clue about any of it. But God had already put all of the pieces together before she ever stepped into the field. She had come to the field of Boaz, the man who would be her kinsman-redeemer, her husband, the father of her child, and the great-grandfather of their great-grandson, King David.

Do you see why this was more than chance?

This was the plan of God.

She went into the fields, hoping to get enough grain to scratch together some dinner. And God gave her not only her daily bread but also a legacy that we would be studying three thousand years later.

Is it possible that He may have something planned for you that you could never imagine? Of course it is. Remember Ephesians 3:20? *"Now to him who is able to do far more abundantly than all that we ask or think."*

A Boaz Man in Plymouth

God had something in mind for a pagan Patuxet Indian named Tisquantum—more than anything he could have ever asked or thought. The Lord would save him from serving idols, turn his heart to Christ, and turn him into a Boaz to save the lives of some English Christians who would lay the foundation for the United States of America. These Christians, who made the dreadful crossing on the tiny Mayflower, had been decimated by sickness and were facing starvation.

Tisquantum, or Squanto as he became known, was captured by Captain George Weymouth and taken from his home in the area that the Pilgrims would name Plymouth. The year was 1605. He was taken to England, where he quickly learned English. For nearly a decade he lived in England, mastering the language and becoming familiar with the English way of life. But he longed to return to his people. Captain John Smith agreed to take him on his voyage to New England and did so, but when Captain Smith put out to sea, another sea captain captured Squanto and some of his tribesman, put them in chains, and took them to North Africa, where he planned on selling them into the slave trade.

In a miraculous way, Squanto was rescued by Christians, heard the gospel, and embraced Jesus Christ. In the next four years, he was able to get back to England and eventually back to his people. He was greatly looking forward to seeing his Patuxet tribe and family. But when he walked into his village after so many years away, he was stunned to find that all of the Patuxet had fallen prey to a plague. Every man, woman, and child had died. All he found were skeletons of the people he loved.

For the next six months, he lived in depression and near despair, feeling that his life was over and had no purpose. This tragic event happened just six months before the Pilgrims landed at Plymouth.

In the providence of God, some six months later, Samoset, an Indian friend from another tribe, told him of this small group of Englishmen who were on the verge of starvation. Squanto immediately agreed to go with Samoset to meet these starving English Pilgrims. When Samoset and his chief returned from the visit, Squanto stayed with the Pilgrims. They had to be absolutely dumbfounded when this intimidating Patuxet Indian walked into camp speaking perfect English.

Peter Marshall and David Manuel told this fascinating story in their wonderful book *The Light and the Glory*. I will let them pick up the rest of the story:

> When Massasoit [the chief] along with his entourage finally left, Squanto stayed. He had found his reason for living. The English were like little babes, so ignorant were they of the ways of the wild. Well, he could certainly do something about that! The next day, he went out and came back with all the eels he could hold in his hands—which the Pilgrims found to be "fat and sweet" and excellent eating. How had he ever caught them? He took several young men with him and taught them how to squash the eels out of the mud with their bare feet, and then catch them with their hands.

But the next thing he showed them was by far the most important, for it would save every one of their lives. April was corn planting month in New England, as well as Virginia. Squanto showed the Pilgrims how to plant corn the Indian way, hoeing six-foot squares in toward the center, putting down four or five kernels, and then fertilizing the corn with fish. At that, the Pilgrims just shook their heads; in four months they had caught exactly one cod. No matter, said Squanto cheerfully; in four days the creeks would be overflowing with fish.

The Pilgrims cast a baleful eye on their amazing friend, who seemed to have adopted them. But Squanto ignored them and instructed the young men how to make the weirs they would need to catch the fish. Obediently, the men did as he told them, and four days later the creeks for miles around were clogged with alewives making their spring run. The Pilgrims did not catch them; they harvested them.[4]

Squanto then carefully instructed and watched the Pilgrims as they planted the corn along with the fish. Then he warned them to set guards throughout the day and the night, because the wolves would smell the fish and come to dig up the corn to get to the fish. For two weeks they must guard the corn! But then he told them that after two weeks they didn't have to worry, because the smell of the decomposing fish would turn the wolves away. And that's exactly what happened.

When the summer months rolled around again, the Pilgrims had twenty acres of healthy corn ready to be harvested.

Squanto was sent by God to save the Mayflower Pilgrims.

Squanto became their Boaz.

God providentially oversaw the entire process. Years before the Pilgrims made their plans to come to America, God was working providentially in the life of a young Indian, ordering his steps through the good and evil of life to turn the evil not only for his good but also for the good of the Pilgrims and the new nation that they would establish.

In regard to Ruth and Naomi, providence ordained their time of arrival, ordained the right benefit, and ordained the right field. And so it was with Squanto and the Pilgrims: providence ordained the time of arrival, the right benefit, and the right field.

In the case of Ruth and Naomi, God brought the women to Boaz. In the case of the Pilgrims, God brought Squanto to them.

Squanto showed up at the right time, showed them the benefits of the eels to feed them and the fish that would soon come to fertilize their corn. And God even brought Squanto to the exact field where they would plant their corn.

So here's the question. Where are you today and what are you facing? Are you so overwhelmed by your circumstances that you're about to lose hope? Are you haunted by the fear that your life is so far gone that it's beyond rescue?

Don't believe it! That is not possible, and Psalm 50:15 (NASB) provides the evidence: "Call upon Me in the day of trouble; and I shall rescue you, and you will honor Me."

As I write these words, America has wallowed in a deep recession for the last several years, and many economists and financial writers are warning that the possibility of a "double-dip" recession is very likely.

In other words, we are living in hard times.

But here's a little bit of perspective. As challenging as these days may be, they are nothing compared to what the Pilgrims faced the day before Squanto showed up.

These Pilgrim men weren't figures out of a Disney movie. These guys were real men with real problems. Many of them had seen their wives and children die on the voyage over from England. More died once they reached land. And the whole community faced imminent starvation because they were completely out of their element in the wild. They were desperate for help to feed their families. And they couldn't run down to the ATM, get some cash, and go over to Walmart to buy some groceries.

They were on their last legs—just like Ruth and Naomi. They had no resources and they were out of options—just like Ruth and Naomi.

Maybe that's where you are as you read these words. In your heart of hearts, you have to face reality. And reality says that you too are on your last legs and just about out of options.

Do you know the Lord Jesus Christ? Do you trust in Him alone to be your Savior? Do you trust in Him to keep His promises? And does it look right now like He has forgotten you?

He hasn't. That's not what He does.

He has saved you, and He will keep on saving you.

He's your Boaz. He's your Savior. He will come through for you—at the right time, with the right benefit, in the right field.

You are reading these words right now in a field. You say no, I'm reading this in my living room. Maybe so, but your living room is part of a house that was built on a field. Are you reading this in your office? Your office was built on what used to be a field. A hundred or more years ago some farmer was trying to eke out a living on the ground that is beneath your feet.

I've got news for you. This entire earth is one big field. And it all belongs to Him. "The earth is the LORD's and the fullness thereof" (Ps. 24:1).

So what's going on in your field? Are you worried? Are you frightened? Are you thinking that you're about finished?

Well, you're not.

The Lord knows you, and He knows where you are. He knows every ounce of pressure that's pushing on your chest and every fear that torments your heart. Google Earth can look at every house and every office in the world. But Google Earth can't look into your heart and fix your life.

But God can, and He will. That's what He does. Right time—right benefit—right field.

"The eyes of the LORD move to and fro throughout the earth that He may strongly support those whose heart is completely His" (2 Chron. 16:9 NASB).

Call on Jesus, the Great Boaz, in your day of trouble. Because of His power and because of His word, He will rescue you, and you will honor Him.

C. H. Spurgeon was right: "Blessed be God, our calamities are matters of time, but our safety is a matter of eternity."

A Boaz Man brings a sense of security, confidence, and affirmation to his family.

CHAPTER NINE

THE MISSING PIECE

"To lengthen my patience is the best way to shorten my troubles."
—George Swinnock

Boaz was a solid citizen, a man with productive land, and a pillar of his community, respected and admired. A well-known man in that part of the country, people would look to him for wisdom and discernment in times of crisis.

As full as his life may have been, however, he was missing a piece.

And what he was missing was a wife and kids.

Before Boaz was ever a gleam in his daddy Salmon's eye, God had planned that he would have a great-grandson by the name of David. Boaz knew nothing about this. God hasn't given us the ability to look down through the generations that follow us.

All Boaz knew was that he was missing a piece. He'd been by himself for many years. Most, if not all, of his childhood friends had been married long ago and probably had kids in their teens. And here was Boaz, still single, still in good health, and probably somewhere around forty—maybe even pushing fifty. We really don't know for sure. But he was no kid, and he was getting some miles on his tires.

I'm sure he had his moments when he figured that if he hadn't met the right woman by now, well, he probably never would. Wouldn't you be thinking that if you were in his sandals? I know I would.

Boaz didn't know it, but that missing piece of his life was about to show up. And if she hadn't shown up at God's perfect time, King David would never have faced off with Goliath in the Valley of Elah. And Solomon would have never written a single proverb or built a temple for the living God on Mount Zion. King Jehoshaphat would have never cried out to God in his distress, led his nation in prayer, or sent the choir out ahead of the army to declare God's victory.

You see, all of this stuff is linked together. God is in the details—all of them.

I'm sure there were days when Boaz wondered why he'd never been able to find a suitable mate to walk through life with him. Believe it or not, he didn't have access to cyberspace dating programs like eHarmony or Match.com. If he was ever to meet a woman, he would have to meet her the old-fashioned way—by actually seeing her and speaking with her. (What a concept!)

But where were the candidates? There were certainly no marriageable women in Bethlehem, and I'm sure that when he went five miles up the road to Jerusalem, he kept his eyes open.

But there had been nothing. No prospects at all.

Or so he imagined.

And why was that? Because God had someone in mind all along. He had a lovely young woman named Ruth waiting in the wings—in Moab of all places. God works strangely!

And all the time Boaz was looking for a suitable woman and no doubt getting frustrated, God was orchestrating his legacy that would include the Son of God being born of a virgin in a stable a thousand years later—not too far from the field where he had planted his barley and wheat.

"My Times Are in Your Hand"

I'm not saying that Boaz was doubled up with anxiety about finding a wife. But I am saying that he was a normal man with normal desires and most likely didn't enjoy setting a supper table for one or sleeping alone every night in his twin bed. The Lord said it Himself! *"It is not good for the man to be alone"* (Gen. 2:18 NASB).

Never has been, never will be.

I think it's a fair guess to assume that Boaz desired a wife and a family. But I don't get the sense that he was going to therapy over it. He seems like the kind of man portrayed in Psalm 31:14–15: "But as for me, I trust in You, O LORD, I say, 'You are my God.' My times are in Your hand" (NASB).

It's mere conjecture on my part, but there may have been moments when Boaz imagined that time had passed him by. But it hadn't passed him by. In fact, his train was just about to pull into the station.

> Now Naomi had a relative of her husband's, a worthy man of the clan of Elimelech, whose name was Boaz. And Ruth the Moabite said to Naomi, "Let me go to the field and glean among the ears of grain after him in whose sight I shall find favor." And she said to her, "Go, my daughter." So she set out and went and gleaned in the field after the reapers, and she happened to come to the part of the field belonging to Boaz, who was of the clan of Elimelech. And

behold, Boaz came from Bethlehem. And he said to the reapers, "The LORD be with you!" And they answered, "The LORD bless you." (Ruth 2:1–4)

We have already established that Boaz was faithful and dependable—both reliable and predictable in his responsibilities. So he showed up for work to see how the harvest was coming, sauntered into the field office with a mug of coffee in hand, and said to the guys, "How's it going?"

No, that's not what he said, because that's not the way they talked back then. He showed up and said to the guys, "The Lord be with you!" And the men replied, "The Lord bless you." And what Boaz didn't know as they exchanged greetings and blessed one another was that he was about to get blessed right out of his field boots.

Everyone would agree that Boaz was already a blessed man, but once again, he was missing a piece.

We throw the term *blessing* around very easily, but what did it actually mean to Boaz in his time? Generally speaking, a blessing from God would encompass the following three areas:

1. Numerous offspring (Gen. 1:28; 9:1)
2. Riches (Gen. 24:35)
3. Victory over enemies (Gen. 27:29; 49:8–12; Deut. 28:7)[1]

Boaz had the land, and it was productive. For that reason, he was a man of wealth. Undoubtedly, during those perilous times in which he lived, he probably had to defend his property and servants from enemies and invaders. We don't read of specific instances where that happened, but it's easy to imagine a man like Boaz taking care of himself rather handily. I can't imagine him backing down in any encounter with enemies, can you?

So, he had wealth and he had victory over his foes.

But he was still alone.

A big piece of his life was still missing, and he wasn't getting any younger. What he was missing was right out of Psalms 127 and 128.

> Behold, children are a heritage from the LORD,
>   the fruit of the womb a reward.
> Like arrows in the hand of a warrior
>   are the children of one's youth.
> Blessed is the man
>   who fills his quiver with them!
> He shall not be put to shame
>   when he speaks with his enemies in the gate.
>   (Ps. 127:3–5)

Boaz was a hard-working man, but when he went home at night after a long day in his fields, there was no one to greet him at the door. His quiver was empty and his house was empty. (I'm guessing he didn't have a dog, either.) He had been blessed in many wonderful ways, but he had no one to share his life with. This was the blessing that was missing in his life. Unless I miss my guess, he was a man who yearned after the hope of Psalm 128:

> Blessed is everyone who fears the LORD,
>   who walks in his ways!
> You shall eat the fruit of the labor of your hands;
>   you shall be blessed, and it shall be well with you.
>
> Your wife will be like a fruitful vine
>   within your house;
> your children will be like olive shoots
>   around your table.
> Behold, thus shall the man be blessed
>   who fears the LORD.

The LORD bless you from Zion!
>   May you see the prosperity of Jerusalem
>   all the days of your life!
> May you see your children's children!
>   Peace be upon Israel!

Boaz, the man of valor, was about to cross paths with a young woman who had just taken refuge under the wings of the God of Israel—a young woman who would take his breath away. And as they interacted, he began to demonstrate the character and behavior of a godly man, a tribal leader, and a staunch citizen who could be counted on in a crisis. I go back to the quote of Leon Morris from the opening chapter of this book:

> The exact expression rendered a mighty man of wealth (AV, RV) is elsewhere translated "a mighty man of valour" (e.g., Judges 11:1). We perhaps get the force of it by thinking of our word "knight". This applied originally to a man distinguished for military prowess, but is now used widely of those whose excellence lies in other fields. In the Old Testament it most often has to do with fighting capacity. Boaz may have been a warrior, for these were troubled times and any man might have to fight. But in this book he appears rather as a solid citizen, a man of influence and integrity in the community and it is likely that this is what the term denotes here.[2]

We're going to see two things working here on parallel tracks. Have you ever been on a train when another train came shooting by, just a few yards away, in the opposite direction? In this case, you're on a train and as you look out the window you see another train just five yards or so away headed in the same direction. You're running in the same direction on parallel tracks.

On one track was the Lord, about to bring Ruth into the life of Boaz and provide his missing piece. On the other track was Boaz and the way he went about handling this major transition in his life. I want you to note the godly and masculine way he conducted himself in this situation. As he dealt with this unforeseen event that began in his field, we will observe his behavior and character traits—especially as it dawned on him that he should become Ruth's kinsman-redeemer.

Yes, Boaz was about to put the moves on Ruth, but he was going to do it in a very respectful, God-honoring way. Nevertheless, he *did move*. He didn't get tied up in knots and become paralyzed over what he should do. He didn't pace around out in the back forty, muttering to himself and kicking dirt clods. No, He moved toward Ruth to find out who she was, and then he took the appropriate steps.

The Masculine Moves of a Godly Man

The first thing that had to be a curveball for Boaz was their age difference. Boaz referred to Ruth in 2:5 as a young woman, and then in verse 8 he called her "my daughter." And right out of the blocks Boaz began to display the traits of godly masculinity as he encountered this young foreign woman from Moab. He saw Ruth gleaning among his workers out in the field, and he had never seen her before. His next steps were active and immediate. There was nothing passive about this guy.

Move 1: Masculine men take appropriate first steps—they aren't passive.

Scripture tells us Boaz engaged in two quick conversations—the first, with his field supervisor:

Then Boaz asked his foreman, "Who is that young woman over there? Who does she belong to?"

And the foreman replied, "She is the young woman from Moab who came back with Naomi. She asked me this morning if she could gather grain behind the harvesters. She has been hard at work ever since, except for a few minutes' rest in the shelter." (Ruth 2:5–7 NLT)

He didn't waste any time, did he? He immediately found out who she was. It piqued his interest even more when he learned that the woman was related to Naomi—whom he certainly knew. Boaz was related to Elimelech before he ever met and married Naomi. So Boaz knew all about Elimelech, his foolish venture into Moab, his death, and the subsequent death of his two boys. And there's no doubt he knew that this young woman was the daughter-in-law of Naomi, recently returned to Bethlehem.

So now that he had the facts, he chewed them over in his mind.

It would be interesting to know what passed through his mind as he processed this information from his supervisor. The young woman was a hard worker—the supervisor made that very clear. And it was interesting that she should suddenly show up in his field on this particular day.

So then he decided to wait for a couple of weeks before he talked to her. Maybe he would run into her at church!

Nope, that's not what he did.

There was no reason to go passive, so he was appropriately active and walked right up to her:

Boaz went over and said to Ruth, "Listen, my daughter. Stay right here with us when you gather grain; don't go to any other fields. Stay right behind the young women working in my field. See which part of the field they are harvesting, and then follow them. I have warned the young men not to treat you roughly. And when you are thirsty, help yourself to the water they have drawn from the well."

Ruth fell at his feet and thanked him warmly. "What have I done to deserve such kindness?" she asked. "I am only a foreigner."

"Yes, I know," Boaz replied. "But I also know about everything you have done for your mother-in-law since the death of your husband. I have heard how you left your father and mother and your own land to live here among complete strangers. May the LORD, the God of Israel, under whose wings you have come to take refuge, reward you fully for what you have done."

"I hope I continue to please you, sir," she replied. "You have comforted me by speaking so kindly to me, even though I am not one of your workers." (Ruth 2:8–13 NLT)

Move 2: Masculine men provide and protect.

After Boaz got the basic information from the field supervisor, he knew that she was Ruth, the girl from Moab, who had come to Bethlehem to live with Naomi. Because he also knew the story, he understood why she was in the field gleaning. Ruth was trying to bring home the grain so that she and Naomi could survive. It was as simple as that.

With that information, he approached her and immediately offered help to lighten her burden. His first act toward her was to provide and protect. So many men make the first move on a woman to see what they can get out of a one-night stand.

There was none of that when Boaz spoke to Ruth.

Here was a godly, masculine man taking the right steps for a vulnerable young woman who was simply trying to live day-to-day. Let's break down what he did.

He told her to stay in his field and not to go to another. He also advised her to stay close to the other women. What he was emphasizing here was safety—he was protecting her. In the next verse he said he had instructed the young men in the field not to touch her. Here was a fact of life: "Gleaning was a potentially dangerous and humiliating task because of the wicked character of some reapers."[3]

Remember that this was the time of the Judges, and "every man did what was right in his own eyes." This was a time of apostasy, chaos, warfare, great spiritual decline in morals, and a widespread decay of civility. In other words, it wasn't a safe time or a safe day for young women to be by themselves. A very quick grisly example of this is found in Judges 19.

A man invited a traveler into his home and the men of the city wanted to have homosexual relations with him. The host said he couldn't do that but offered them his virgin daughter and his concubine. The men said no—they wanted the visitor. He finally sent his concubine out, and the men raped her throughout the night. Then her master retrieved her in the morning, killed her, cut her body into twelve pieces, and sent them to the scattered tribes throughout Israel.

As horrific as that piece of history is, it sheds light on how wicked and dangerous the culture had become.

So a godly man—a masculine man—who would step up and give protection to a young woman was a rare man indeed! And in the next breath, he offered her the provision of water. The sun blazed hot in the late spring in Bethlehem. It was a task and a chore for a young woman to leave the field, go find water, and then make her way back into the field. The conveniences of life so easily accessible to us were unknown back then. No water fountains for the gleaners, no bottled water. It was a task to get to water on top of the task of gleaning grain. So he offered her the water that had been provided for the workers, whom he had ordered not to bother Ruth either verbally or physically.

You can imagine what a gift Boaz was to the young foreign woman standing in a foreign field trying to gather enough grain to make some dinner for her and her mother-in-law. You can imagine how heartfelt was her response:

Ruth fell at his feet and thanked him warmly. "What have I done to deserve such kindness?" she asked. "I am only a foreigner."

She was blown away by this man. He didn't make any inappropriate comments or advances as so many men would do—he was simply there to offer her his help, protection, and provision.

And Ruth? She was utterly at a loss to understand why he would be so kind.

At that point, of course, Ruth didn't have a clue who this man was, other than a random Israelite landowner. She didn't know his position, his character, or the fact that he was blood relative to her dead husband. But he was about to clue her in. He told her who he was and that he knew the family's entire story. He knew that she had come to know the Lord, had returned to Bethlehem with Naomi, and he honored her for her decisions and her support of Naomi.

At this point, Ruth had to be somewhat stunned.

She was probably expecting to be given a rough time in the fields, yet here was a man complimenting her, providing for her, and protecting her.

And then … he invited her to lunch.

At mealtime Boaz called to her, "Come over here, and help yourself to some food. You can dip your bread in the sour wine." So she sat with his harvesters, and Boaz gave her some roasted grain to eat. She ate all she wanted and still had some left over.

When Ruth went back to work again, Boaz ordered his young men, "Let her gather grain right among the sheaves without stopping her. And pull out some heads of barley from the bundles and drop them on purpose for her. Let her pick them up, and don't give her a hard time!"

> So Ruth gathered barley there all day, and when she
> beat out the grain that evening, it filled an entire basket.
> (Ruth 2:14–17 NLT)

Not only did Boaz invite Ruth to lunch, but he also made sure she had plenty to eat. In fact, he gave her so much that she had food left over. In her mind, she had no business being at that lunch in the first place. But Boaz had invited her and it was apparent that she was his special guest. And if there was any doubt about that, when she went back to work, Boaz told his work crew to pull out some extra bundles of barley to give to her. Some translations use the word *ephah* to describe what the extra amounts actually amounted to—approximately six gallons by measure or thirty pounds by weight.

Once again, Boaz was stepping up to the plate by providing for her—and don't forget the protecting part. The young men were under strict orders from the boss not to bother her in any way. So here was a young widow, in a foreign land, in a foreign field, on her first day of trying to scratch out a living, and she ran into a godly man who protected her, spoke kindly to her, invited her back, forbade anyone to harass her, gave her all the water she needed, offered her lunch, and then sent her home with thirty pounds of grain.

Suddenly this young woman, who was only attempting to stay out of the poor house, found herself trying to figure out where to store the surplus. And it's all because she ran into the right kind of man.

Boaz was a protector and a provider. That's what a godly man is. And as one commentator pointed out, this was probably the first kind thing that anyone had done for Ruth since her husband had died back in Moab. In fact, it may have been the first time in her life that she truly saw a man who could be trusted.

The reason for that is simple. Ruth was from Moab, and Moab was a cruel and horrific place. The people of Moab didn't worship the God of

Boaz. They worshipped Chemosh, and the god that you worship makes a difference in the men of the nation and in the nation itself. John Phillips explained:

> Ruth was a Moabitess, a member of an accursed race. She was born and bred in paganism. The gods of her people were fearful, filthy, demon gods.... The priests of Moab were powerful and cruel, and they served an assortment of gods. But the most feared god of all was Chemosh, who had his terrible place among the gentler gods of a platform of movable stones under which great fires could be kindled. Chemosh's lap was so constructed that little children placed on its red-hot surface would roll down a declined plane into his fiery belly while slaves kept fresh fagots heaped on the hungry fires.
>
> When disaster threatened Moab—plague, famine, the possibility of war—the priests called for another burning. They would come around the homes to inspect children, looking for possible victims, especially firstborn sons. With a red dye obtained from the seashore, they would stain the wrists of designated victims. There was no court of appeal from the priest's decision. Children with stained wrists were doomed to horrible deaths.
>
> Perhaps when Ruth was a child, she would hear her parents whispering about this and her heart would be filled with dreadful dreams that would be transformed into nightmares.
>
> When Ruth was old enough to play with other girls she heard about another god—actually a fertility goddess who offered the Moabites regeneration through the gratification of lust with harlot priestesses in the temple. The fertility

of fields and farms, people believed, depended on the sex orgies in her temple.

Just as the priests kept their eyes open for firstborn sons that could be fed to Chemosh, [the priests of the fertility goddess] kept their lustful eyes open for promising girls who could be conscripted for the foul trade of the temple.[4]

Boys and girls in Moab weren't protected. Moab wasn't a safe place, because their gods were demonic.

This was Ruth's nation. Her background was one of fear and never feeling safe. And then on one eventful morning, she met Boaz in a field. He was a man who trusted in the one true God, Yahweh. This great God of Israel was good: the Lord is good and does good (Ps. 119:68). And when this great God got a hold on a man's life, He would turn that man into someone who could be trusted. Boaz was a trustworthy man. God had changed his heart. So when he met Ruth, he wasn't thinking of how he could take advantage of her. He was only concerned about doing what was best for her and helping her out of a tight spot.

And his first inclination was to provide and protect.

He wanted her to know that she was in his field and that she was safe. She didn't have to worry about the young men sexually harassing her. She didn't need to concern herself about finding enough food and water to get her through the day. She didn't need to be anxious about finding enough grain to take care of her mother-in-law. Boaz made sure that she would go home with thirty pounds of grain.

Now that you know where Ruth came from, do you see how staggered she must have been with this man who stepped up to protect and provide for her? It very well could have been the first time in her life that she had ever met such a man. But what made Boaz different was his God—this God that she too had embraced.

At the end of the day, when she made her way back to Naomi, she had to be walking as if in a dream. On her very first day seeking a place to glean, she had met a man who was safe—a man who protected her and provided for her. And he had given her an open invitation to come back each day. She could hardly believe it. She was in a strange land but she was *safe*. And ultimately, she was safe because of the God who ruled the land—and the God who ruled Boaz.

All of those years when she was vulnerable in Moab and without knowledge of the one true God, she was being protected and preserved for Boaz. She was the missing piece of Boaz's life. But she wasn't missing from the eye of the Lord. He had His eye on her before she was born. He was the One who kept her from the demonic priests who served the demonic gods. And it all came into HD focus that one day in the field when Boaz showed up.

The pieces finally starting to fall into place.

Every one of them.

A Boaz Man is a source of wisdom and perspective in a time of crisis.

CHAPTER TEN

MAN IN MOTION

"Christ's performances outstrip his promises."
—Nehemiah Rogers

Three weeks after meeting Mary for the first time, I asked her to marry me. Ten months later we were married, and we're still going strong and coming up on thirty-five years of marriage.

I don't necessarily recommend our method. But it really wasn't our method in the first place. It was the surprising and unexpected providence of God. Almost immediately, He began putting the pieces together, and both Mary and I knew it.

And isn't it strange to think that we met in a barley field....

Actually, we didn't. We met in a class on marriage and family—but I was looking for a transition back into Ruth and Boaz, who *did* meet in a barley field.

When the barley harvest and the wheat harvest were finally coming to an end, a period of roughly four to five months after their first meeting in the field, things started moving rapidly. And once again, I want to observe the traits of a godly, masculine man who senses that God is at work in his life. I want to note how Boaz responded to each situation he encountered as he moved toward marriage with Ruth.

After Ruth had the amazing meeting with Boaz, she went home and related all the events of the day to Naomi. You can just imagine Naomi saying, "Tell me everything—don't leave out a thing!" So Naomi put the tea kettle on the stove, and Ruth poured out the whole story of the encounter with Boaz and his remarkable kindness and favor toward her (Ruth 2:17–23).

As Ruth related the details (as only a woman can), Naomi sat listening, both ears open, taking it all in. After processing it all, you can imagine the joy beginning to dawn on her face. In that moment, she looked more like Naomi (pleasant) again, rather than Mara (bitter). In verse 20 she said, "May he be blessed by the LORD, whose kindness has not forsaken the living or the dead!" Then she added, "The man is a close relative of ours, one of our redeemers."

It's as though Naomi suddenly saw where all of this was going. She immediately saw this not as a chance occurrence but as a kindness (*hesed*) of the living God. This was too good to be true! Only God could have arranged this—and here's the rest of story.

This Boaz was one of the family's potential kinsman-redeemers! Undoubtedly, Naomi began to see how this was more than a chance meeting. The conversation went on, with Ruth speaking first:

> "Besides, he said to me, 'You shall keep close by my young
> men until they have finished all my harvest.'" And Naomi

said to Ruth, her daughter-in-law, "It is good, my daughter, that you go out with his young women, lest in another field you be assaulted." So she kept close to the young women of Boaz, gleaning until the end of the barley and wheat harvests. And she lived with her mother-in-law. (Ruth 2:21–23)

Naomi encouraged Ruth to accept the invitation of Boaz and to work and glean only in his field. The barley harvest started in early March and ran through April, followed by the wheat harvest, which began in early June and lasted through July. That means that Ruth and Boaz met in his field in early March and she continued to work with his servants and interact with him on a regular basis through July. And the whole time, Naomi was watching very carefully.

March through July is roughly five months—nearly half a year. And nothing further had happened between Ruth and Boaz. At least, nothing that Naomi could see. So here's when she conjured up a plan that was one of the most confusing in all of the Bible. The very next verse introduces the story:

Then Naomi her mother-in-law said to her, "My daughter, should I not seek rest for you, that it may be well with you? Is not Boaz our relative, with whose young women you were? See, he is winnowing barley tonight at the threshing floor. Wash therefore and anoint yourself, and put on your cloak and go down to the threshing floor, but do not make yourself known to the man until he has finished eating and drinking. But when he lies down, observe the place where he lies. Then go and uncover his feet and lie down, and he will tell you what to do." And she replied, "All that you say I will do." (Ruth 3:1–5)

It's been an interesting year for us as a family. Each of our three children was married within nine months of one another. What a whirlwind—and what a great time.

I have one daughter and two sons. Someone asked me after Rachel's wedding what it was like to marry off a daughter. I replied that it was a privilege, because she had been led to such an outstanding young man. Court was the right guy for Rachel. So it was a great wedding that Saturday night in September. What a time, what a ceremony that honored the Lord, and what a reception/dinner afterward under the big white tent.

And then I filed for bankruptcy on Monday morning.

Just kidding....

But that was just the first of three weddings. Each one was a blast because Rachel, John, and Josh had found godly mates. And all three of my children have their own unique providential stories. And none of them got engaged after three weeks! That would have given me a heart attack.

I well remember the night that it was apparent that Court was the man for Rachel. So I told her to go to the spa, get all spruced up, and then go to Court's apartment at midnight, and lie down at his feet.

Are you kidding me?

There's no way in the world any of us would have given that counsel to our daughters! Nor would our wives. So what in the world was Naomi thinking? What was she smoking?

To back up a little, what was Naomi's motivation in the first place? Bible scholars are split on this. Some think that Naomi was simply following the custom of the time, in sending Ruth in to meet Boaz in the middle of the night. It was her attempt to bring about an arranged marriage. The New Living Translation of Ruth 3:1 renders the verse like this: "'My daughter, it's time that I found a permanent home for you.'" So Naomi's thinking was that she had to go to bat for Ruth and find her a husband and get her settled in life.

The other view is that you never see this custom anywhere else in Scripture. In other words, this wasn't a custom but Naomi's way of trying to light a fire under Boaz so that he would marry Ruth. They had met months earlier in the field during the start of the barley harvest, and there was a definite connection. But the weeks went by and the barley harvest was complete, then right behind it came the wheat harvest. Ruth continued to glean in Boaz's field, and undoubtedly the connection was not going away.

But apparently Boaz wasn't moving fast enough for Naomi.

So she devised a plan to get the show on the road.

I'm sure she was well-meaning in her motivation, but some feel that she got ahead of the Lord just a little bit. Have you ever done that? Right … and so have I. I think she was so excited about the possibility of Ruth's marrying Boaz that she just had to step in and help the situation along. In other words, instead of trusting the Holy Spirit, she was going to become the junior Holy Spirit.

But here's a newsflash. The Holy Spirit doesn't need any help.

Sometimes we forget that fact, don't we? And in this case, it seems that Naomi devised a plan that quite frankly wasn't all that wise.

But even as she put together this unusual approach and arrangement, she was counting on one thing: *Boaz could be trusted*.

In Ruth 2:4, Naomi told Ruth to go lie down at Boaz's feet while he was sleeping, and she told her to do whatever he instructed her to do. Do you think she would have said this if she'd any doubts at all about Boaz's character? I don't think so. Do you think if he was known as a regular down at the singles bar she would have told Ruth to do whatever he told her to do? No way. It was an iffy plan by a desperate woman lacking sense, but at least she knew that Boaz was a wise and godly man. He would not take advantage. He would not be anything less than honorable. He was a man of valor. He was the best of all the men in Bethlehem and the surrounding cities. He was Boaz. And Boaz could be trusted—even in a somewhat precarious situation.

It always comes down to the character of the man. Not his reputation, but his *character*. Some men work very hard on reputation and image. They want to look trustworthy. Ironically, these are the very ones who end up showing a deficiency in character.

Men of character are concerned about their reputations too, but they know that the best way to obtain an honorable reputation is by developing honest character.

I recently read a fascinating modern-day Ruth-and-Boaz memoir written by Carolyn Weber. The title is *Surprised by Oxford*, and it's the story of a young woman who went to Oxford to get an education, met a young Christian man who continually disturbed her yet attracted her at the same time, and then eventually came to Christ and married the young man.

In one of their first meetings, they were attempting to cross a street full of traffic. She immediately realized as they crossed the street that he had positioned himself between her and the oncoming cars. In other words, he had taken her arm to protect her. And then once on the sidewalk, he very subtly positioned himself closer to the curb, where any errant cyclists would undoubtedly strike him instead of her.

He didn't say a word about any of this, but this very bright young woman quickly figured it out. And she turned on him in anger and proceeded to tell him in no uncertain words that she didn't *need* to be protected. She could cross the traffic without his help. In response, he agreed wholeheartedly and respectfully that indeed she could navigate traffic without his help. In exasperation she asked him why he had done it. And he replied that "it was the right thing to do." That really set her off!

I enjoyed reading this well-written true story of how a brilliant young woman from a loving but broken family encountered for the first time in her life a true, strong, masculine, and godly man. She had a father who was very gifted and very unpredictable. He walked away from the family and left them destitute. He would reappear from time to time, expecting their love and respect, but they were all exhausted from trying to pay the rent and buy groceries—something he failed to do. She had grown up learning not to trust men. And then she ran into this young man she described as TDH: tall, dark, and handsome.

I enjoyed this book immensely because I knew this young man when he was SDH: short, dark, and handsome. The first time I met him I was walking out of the seminary academic building with his dad, my friend, Stu Weber. Kent must have been three or four years old. He was dark and good looking—but as I remember he was about 3'5". Now he's 6'5".

Later in the story, she apologized to him for her behavior in the traffic, and then as they talked further, she opened up to him, because she trusted him, and told him about her father. She told him about her mother working hours and hours to feed her abandoned family and how she labored to make straight As in high school to get a college scholarship—on top of working full time and surviving on three to four hours of sleep at night.

Sobbing, she told him she would never trust men, because they couldn't be trusted. Fathers, boyfriends, all of them make promises and then run away, never to be seen again—unless they want something. She began to pound his chest with her fists. And then he held her hands, looked gently into her eyes, and said,

> Not all men are like the ones you describe. Unfortunately, many are. But many are not.… That is not my father. Or my grandfather. Or my brothers. Or any of the men I know and respect as close friends. That's not me, either. Nobody is perfect, but I know lots of men who strive very hard to be the real thing, who know God intimately and answer to something far greater than themselves. They are men who are humble, who respect women, devote themselves in marriage and families. They are men whose genuine, disciplined lives model God's goodness in a myriad of ways. These men, they exist.[1]

TDH could say that because he comes from a line of Boaz Men. I've known his dad and his grandfather for close to forty years. I would trust them with anything I have, including my family. They have proven themselves trustworthy.

Naomi may have been wrong in her approach, but she knew this Boaz guy could be trusted in any situation—even in one where most men would have taken advantage. He was the real deal. He would know what to do. And Naomi was right.

Boaz honored and respected women. Therefore, Ruth would be safe.

So what happened when Boaz rolled over to adjust his pillow in the middle of the night?

> So she went down to the threshing floor and did according to all that her mother-in-law had commanded her. When Boaz had eaten and drunk and his heart was merry, he went to lie down at the end of the heap of grain; and she came secretly, and uncovered his feet and lay down. It happened in the middle of the night that the man was startled and bent forward; and behold, a woman was lying at his feet. He said, "Who are you?" And she answered, "I am Ruth your maid. So spread your covering over your maid, for you are a close relative." Then he said, "May you be blessed of the LORD, my daughter. You have shown your last kindness to be better than the first by not going after young men, whether poor or rich. Now, my daughter, do not fear. I will do for you whatever you ask, for all my people in the city know that you are a woman of excellence. Now it is true I am a close relative; however, there is a relative closer than I. Remain this night, and when morning comes, if he will redeem you, good; let him redeem you. But if he does not wish to redeem you, then I will redeem you, as the LORD lives. Lie down until morning." (Ruth 3:6–13 NASB)

There is nothing more uncomfortable than an awkward situation. Boaz faced an awkward situation in the middle of the night when he woke and Ruth was lying at his feet. She was lovely and perfumed. He was a godly and mature man who had been single all of his life. He was not used to waking up in middle of the night with a young widow at the foot of his bed.

There's no getting around it—it was awkward.

Ruth was there because her mother-in-law, Naomi, had told her this was what she should do. Naomi had orchestrated this entire awkward situation. I'm sure she didn't intend for it to be problematic. But it was. It was problematic for Boaz as he came out of a deep sleep and discovered a desirable young woman at his feet. And it's awkward for us as we try to figure out what in the world was going on.

I should say something up front because it's the obvious question. Did something sexual take place in this meeting that Naomi orchestrated? The answer is no. Something sexual easily could have resulted, but it's very clear that nothing of the sort occurred. And that was all because of the maturity, wisdom, and character of Boaz.

In this incident, Boaz demonstrated how awkward and cumbersome situations are to be handled by godly men. He did nothing to take advantage of Ruth. He was aboveboard and without sin in his interaction with her. She didn't belong to him, and she wasn't his to take.

Naomi knew that because of the family relationship Boaz could be the kinsman-redeemer for Ruth. In Naomi's mind, he was the logical candidate to be Ruth's husband. But Boaz knew that there was another man who was the first in line to be Ruth's kinsman-redeemer. Either Naomi in concocting her plan didn't know it, or she did know it and tried to get around it. But Boaz was an honorable man, and he wouldn't shortcut the process. Undoubtedly he had thought about Ruth becoming his wife, but in the levirate law and customs of the day, another man was in line before him. This apparently was the reason Boaz had not made any further moves toward Ruth.

Here's a principle about Boaz Men: *they go through the right chan-nels*. In other words, Boaz was a man of character and he refused to take shortcuts. He was going to do this the right way and go through the right channels. It was an unusual situation he would handle according to scriptural principles.

And what was the principle? The principle at play here is in Deuteronomy 25:5–10, and it was referred to as levirate law.

> The word "levirate" comes from the Latin word *levir*, which means a brother-in-law, although it is possible that the prin-ciple of levirate law extended beyond that relationship. The principle underlying the levirate law was the importance of the continuity of the family line. Not only was life sacred, and the land sacred, but the continuity of God's covenant promises and the fulfillment from generation to generation was important. The levirate law stated that if a husband died childless, his brother (i.e. his widow's brother-in-law) would then father a son for the dead man.[2]

Sinclair Ferguson continued that thought and observed:

> There is ongoing debate about whether or not Naomi is thinking specifically here of levirate marriage, since Boaz is certainly not a brother-in-law. But the principles of God's laws were never limited merely to the strict letter and it is possible that the provision was interpreted and applied more broadly.[3]

If Boaz was going to step in, marry Ruth, and assume responsibility for Ruth, then he was going to do it right. No quick fixes and no hanging threads. He was going to legally cross his t's and dot his i's.

There was apparently a lot more to this than either Naomi or Ruth was aware of. So briefly—in a whisper next to her ear there on the threshing floor—he sketched out the facts for Ruth. There was another man who stood first in line, but Boaz would go talk to him.

In essence, he promised this young woman, "If this man doesn't step up and assume the responsibility as your kinsman-redeemer, I will. Count on it." He made the pledge and the promise, but he didn't touch her. Early in the morning, he sent her away with a gift for her and Naomi: enough grain to feed an army for a month!

When Naomi heard the story, she was content to wait for God's outcome. She knew this man Boaz and was quietly confident that he wouldn't waste time wringing his hands and trying to decide if he could make a commitment.

Not Boaz!

He would be up at first light, heading for the courthouse.

And so he was.

> So she lay at his feet until the morning, but arose before one could recognize another. And he said, "Let it not be known that the woman came to the threshing floor." And he said, "Bring the garment you are wearing and hold it out." So she held it, and he measured out six measures of barley and put it on her. Then she went into the city. And when she came to her mother-in-law, she said, "How did you fare, my daughter?" Then she told her all that the man had done for her, saying, "These six measures of barley he gave to me, for he said to me, 'You must not go back empty-handed to your mother-in-law.'" She replied, "Wait, my daughter, until you learn how the matter turns out, for the man will not rest but will settle the matter today." (Ruth 3:14–18)

In football terms, this is a play that shouldn't have been called. It wasn't in the divine playbook. You might even call it a "broken play." Nevertheless, Naomi called the play, thinking she was doing the right thing. And so Boaz woke up, realized what had happened, and knew that the ball was now in his hands.

In other words, he had to improvise, just like an experienced NFL quarterback does when there's a broken play. If you've watched much football, you've seen it happen a hundred times. A receiver gets mixed up and runs a wrong route, a running back breaks left instead of right, or a linebacker breaks through the offensive line untouched. That's when the leadership of a quarterback is tested. He's a man on the move, evading tackles, reading the situation, checking down his receivers, and using his wisdom and experience on the fly to find the best possible solution to rectify a broken situation.

Now Boaz had gone up to the gate and sat down there. And behold, the redeemer, of whom Boaz had spoken, came by. So Boaz said, "Turn aside, friend; sit down here." And he turned aside and sat down. And he took ten men of the elders of the city and said, "Sit down here." So they sat down. Then he said to the redeemer, "Naomi, who has come back from the country of Moab, is selling the parcel of land that belonged to our relative Elimelech. So I thought I would tell you of it and say, 'Buy it in the presence of those sitting here and in the presence of the elders of my people.' If you will redeem it, redeem it. But if you will not, tell me, that I may know, for there is no one besides you to redeem it, and I come after you." And he said, "I will redeem it." Then Boaz said, "The day you buy the field from the hand of Naomi, you also acquire Ruth the Moabite, the widow of the dead, in order to perpetuate the name of the dead in his inheritance." Then the redeemer said, "I cannot redeem it for myself, lest I impair my own inheritance. Take my right of redemption yourself, for I cannot redeem it." (Ruth 4:1–6)

Here's another Boaz principle: *godly leaders don't hesitate to take necessary first steps.*

First thing that morning, Boaz got a cup of coffee and headed to the title company to sign the papers. Actually that's not what he did. He went to the city gates, which functioned like the courthouse, and kept his eyes peeled for the man he needed to see. In God's providence, the man came walking along before Boaz had a chance to finish his coffee.

Boaz invited the man to sit, turned to the elders, and stated his business. Here's another principle: *Boaz Men are straight up and honest.* He didn't try to slant the situation in his favor. He just laid the facts out on the table. He told the nearest relative that the land of Elimelech was going to be sold by Naomi. Did the man want the land? Yes was the response. Boaz came back with the next fact, which was if this man were to buy the land, he had to marry Ruth as well and have children with her to continue the family line. When the man heard this he balked. He then yielded the right to Boaz.

And it was almost a done deal.

Since title companies hadn't been invented yet, the two men just used a sandal (saving a bundle on attorney fees).

Now in those days it was the custom in Israel for anyone transferring a right of purchase to remove his sandal and hand it to the other party. This publicly validated the transaction. So the other family redeemer drew off his sandal as he said to Boaz, "You buy the land."

Then Boaz said to the elders and to the crowd standing around, "You are witnesses that today I have bought from Naomi all the property of Elimelech, Kilion, and Mahlon.

And with the land I have acquired Ruth, the Moabite widow of Mahlon, to be my wife. This way she can have a son to carry on the family name of her dead husband and to inherit the family property here in his hometown. You are all witnesses today."

Then the elders and all the people standing in the gate replied, "We are witnesses! May the LORD make this woman who is coming into your home like Rachel and Leah, from whom all the nation of Israel descended! May you prosper in Ephrathah and be famous in Bethlehem. And may the LORD give you descendants by this young woman who will be like those of our ancestor Perez, the son of Tamar and Judah." (Ruth 4:7–12 NLT)

It was the custom in these times to seal the deal with a sandal. And so they did. It was clean, legal, legitimate, and it honored the Lord. And it could never be questioned.

Boaz took Naomi's broken play, scrambled, and turned it into a touchdown. He didn't cheat, didn't make a backroom deal, and nobody got a kickback. Everybody read the bill before signing it. It was public before the ten elders, and the Lord approved it.

Now Boaz, a man who thought he would never have a family, was about to enjoy amazing grace. He had no doubt thought that he'd be alone for the rest of his days, but that was not to be.

So Boaz took Ruth, and she became his wife. And he went in to her, and the LORD gave her conception, and she bore a son. Then the women said to Naomi, "Blessed be the LORD, who has not left you this day without a redeemer, and may his name be renowned in Israel! He shall be to you a restorer of life and a nourisher of your old age, for your daughter-in-law who loves you, who is more to you than seven sons, has given birth to him." Then Naomi took the child and laid him on her lap and became his nurse. And the women of the neighborhood gave him a name, saying, "A son has been born to Naomi." They named him Obed. He was the father of Jesse, the father of David. (Ruth 4:13–17)

Boaz had been used to living alone. In the blink of an eye, he had a wife who crowded him in bed, a mother-in-law in the next bedroom, and before long he had to add on another bedroom for the nursery. He never thought he would see the day. I've got to believe that Boaz was amazed at how quickly his life had changed.

Naomi had lost all the men in her life. Now she had Boaz and a grandson.

Ruth was a foreign woman who had known fear all of her life. She couldn't trust the men or the priests of Moab because they viewed women as objects—or mere sacrifices to the demonic gods. But now she had been redeemed by Yahweh, the one true God of Israel and by one of his choice men in Bethlehem, the mighty man of valor, Boaz.

She was blessed beyond her wildest dreams, but the Lord wasn't done yet.

The Lord would continue to bless the legacy of Boaz and Ruth as the centuries rolled by. A hundred years or so down the line, their great-grandson, David, would become the king of Israel. He too would be born in Bethlehem. But the greatest gift of all would be another descendant who would come a thousand years later and be born to a virgin in a little stable—also in Bethlehem. He would be the Messiah, the Lord Jesus Christ, the ultimate Boaz, the Savior, for all who call upon His name.

What a great God we serve. He encloses us behind and before. We live in our present chapter of history, but He was working in our lives in the previous generation and chapters, and He will continue to work in the coming generations and chapters:

> Now these are the generations of Perez: Perez fathered
> Hezron, Hezron fathered Ram, Ram fathered Amminadab,
> Amminadab fathered Nahshon, Nahshon fathered Salmon,
> Salmon fathered Boaz, Boaz fathered Obed, Obed fathered
> Jesse, and Jesse fathered David. (Ruth 4:18–22)

The family line of Boaz became the greatest family in the history of Israel … and of all peoples and all time.

What a man Boaz was and what a family he had! You may be reading this and wishing that you had such an honorable family. Perhaps you look back over your family and hang your head in shame. Don't be too quick to regret your roots. Who knows? The Lord may have plans for your family that are beyond your wildest dreams.

We are told in Ruth 4:21 that the father of Boaz was Salmon. We don't know much about Salmon, but what we do know from Matthew 1:5 is that he and his wife married and were blessed with a little boy named Boaz. Do you know the name of the woman who married Salmon and bore a son named Boaz?

Her name was Rahab.

She was the prostitute in Jericho who protected the two spies sent in by Joshua to spy out the land. She too became wonderfully converted and followed the Lord God of Israel.

What a wretched, sordid background she had. But she met a great Savior who created the worlds and forgave sinners. He cleaned up her heart and life and gave her a godly husband, and they produced a godly man who was a rock in an unstable time in an unstable land.

The Lord reaches down and saves sinners. And then He grows them in grace and in His Word. It doesn't matter where you have been or what you have done. It's doesn't matter where your family is from or what shame is in your generational past. The Lord Jesus Christ is a great Savior.

He's the great Boaz.

And if you will turn to Him in your moment of need, He will be your great Redeemer—forever—and to future generations yet to be born in your family line.

A Boaz Man doesn't hesitate to take necessary first steps.

THE ENDURING QUALITIES OF A BOAZ MAN

✪ A Boaz Man follows the Great Shepherd and shepherds his family.

✪ A Boaz Man reveals his true character in a crisis.

✪ A Boaz Man rides out the hard times while trusting in the goodness of God.

✪ A Boaz Man refuses to run ahead of the Lord.

✪ A Boaz Man trusts the Lord for daily provision.

✪ A Boaz Man remembers that God brings very good things out of very bad things.

✪ A Boaz Man looks for the breakthrough in every setback.

✪ A Boaz Man brings a sense of security, confidence, and affirmation to his family.

✪ A Boaz Man is a source of wisdom and perspective in a time of crisis.

✪ A Boaz Man doesn't hesitate to take necessary first steps.

Study Questions for Personal Reflection or Group Discussion

Chapter 1: Boaz Man

1. Owen Strachan said, "The gospel does not kill pleasure or aggressiveness. Rather, as [Jonathan] Edwards has shown, it frees Christians to experience true pleasure and to act in manly ways for a far greater cause than ourselves." What is true pleasure? How does the gospel free us to experience true pleasure? What is the far greater cause? What are some manly ways of serving that cause?

2. The difference between white bread men and whole grain men is whether they have the substance to stay the course and take care of their families in the stress of life. How can you tell if a man has substance? For instance, how does he relate to money? To work? To women? To his children? To disappointment? To dreams and desires?

3. Jeremiah Burroughs said that in God's providence, many future things that you're unaware of may depend on a circumstance that currently seems hard to understand. What is one thing about your life right now that you

have trouble being content with? How does your view of God's providence affect the way you look at your situation?

4. In this chapter the author said, "God has a detailed and providential plan that He is working in your life—even when it seems like your life is dull and boring." How would your life change if you fully believed this? How do you usually deal with the boring parts of life?

5. Boaz's influence in his community came mainly from his character, not his bank account or his fascinating personality. What's the difference between personality and character? Do you think it's possible to be influential today if you have strong character but only average personality and a small bank account? If so, in what ways is it possible? If not, why isn't it possible?

6. What are some ways your situation calls you to look out for the interests of others, not just yourself? What are the challenges you face in doing that? What help do you need from Jesus to be the kind of man who consistently looks out for others' interests?

Chapter 2: White Bread Gone Bad

1. What qualities of A. P. Giannini do you admire? How does your life call for each of those qualities?

2. The period of the judges was a time when "there was no king in Israel. Everyone did what was right in his own eyes" (Judg. 21:25). What's wrong with doing what's right in your own eyes? In practical terms, how does a man go about breaking that habit? What are some steps he can take? What help does he need?

3. Thomas Watson said, "The moralist's religion is all in the leaf; it consists only in the externals, but godliness is a holy sap which is rooted in the soul." If a man wants to acquire the habit of doing what is right in God's eyes, how does he keep that from being just a matter of externals? How does something like that get rooted in the soul?

4. Respond to this statement from Peter Marshall: "Once and for all, we must put out of our minds that the purpose of life here is to enjoy ourselves.... That is not what life is about. You were put here for a purpose, and that purpose is not related to superficial pleasures.... You do not have a right to happiness. You have a right to nothing." What do you see as the purpose of your life? How do you respond to the idea that you don't have a right to happiness?

5. Do you believe America is in decline because God has given the nation over to a mind that worships self and resists truth? If not, in what ways do you disagree with this analysis? If so, how do you think God wants you to live in this situation? Is God calling you to leave the nation physically, withdraw into a protective cocoon, or what?

6. If God is overseeing the entire process that gets food to your table, how does that affect the way you approach mealtimes? The way you approach work? The way you sleep at night?

Chapter 3: Area 51

1. Have you ever made a decision that you look back on now and can't believe how stupid you were? If so, what was your attitude toward God at the time? What did you learn about yourself and God from that experience?

2. Matthew Henry said, "It is an evidence of a discontented, distrustful, unstable spirit, to be weary of the place in which God has set us, and to be leaving it immediately whenever we meet with any uneasiness or inconvenience in it." How can we tell the difference between wanting to leave a place because we're discontented and wanting to leave because God is calling us to move on?

3. What are some ways men respond when their goals are blocked? What does God want us to do when our goals are blocked?

4. Make a list of your life expectations. Write down what you honestly expect from your wife (or the women in your life if you're not married), your kids (if you have them), your boss, your coworkers, your church, your friends, God. Who can you share that list with—who is someone you can trust to give you constructive feedback? (If you're meeting with a group, you can allow ten minutes of quiet to get as far as you can on your individual lists. Then talk about what it's like to look at that list of expectations.)

5. What challenges do you face in balancing the demands of your work and the needs of your family? What helps you deal with that?

6. In this chapter the author said, "Work for the Lord, honor Him as best you know how, and leave the responses of people in authority over you to Him." How are you affected by the responses of people in authority over you? What do you do when the responses are negative?

7. Do you ever feel like leaving your current job to do full-time ministry? Why or why not? What do you think God is saying in all of that?

Chapter 4: Rock or Sand

1. Navy SEAL Eric Greitens says this of most men who survive SEAL training: "Even in great pain, faced with the test of their lives, they had the ability to step outside of their own pain, put aside their own fear and ask: How can I help the guy next to me?" Why do you suppose this ability is so crucial to a man's success in a hard place?

2. What voices in our world tell us we can control our future? What specifics in this chapter motivate you to reject those voices and trust God with your future?

3. "Failure is the opportunity to begin again more intelligently." How is that like or unlike the ways you have responded to failure in the past? What do you think about this attitude toward failure? Why?

4. Read Isaiah 65:2 and picture God with His arms open, ready to welcome you back if you've gone off course. How does that picture compare with your usual picture of God?

5. Why did John Newton believe it was merciful for God to train us by disappointing our plans? How do you respond to his argument?

6. Why is a godly support system so important for you? For your family? What can you do to make sure that you and your family have and retain a strong support system?

Chapter 5: Keep Calm and Carry On

1. What are some Moabs a man might be tempted to run to when times are hard? How does each of those Moabs lead to worse problems?

2. What reasons for trusting God did Jehoshaphat give in 2 Chronicles 20:5–13? What do you think could lead a man who believes those things to later make an alliance with people who do bad things?

3. C. H. Spurgeon wrote, "A daily portion is *all that a man really wants*. We do not need tomorrow's supplies; that day has not yet dawned, and its wants are as yet unborn.... Enough is not only as good as a feast, but it is all that the glutton can truly enjoy. *That is all that we should expect*; a craving for more than this is ungrateful. When our Father does not give us more, we should be content with his daily allowance." How do you measure what is enough? Is a daily portion enough for you? Why or why not?

4. Read Matthew 6:25–34. What in this passage can help a man stay calm and carry on in hard times? Is there anything in this passage that is challenging for you to hang on to? If so, what?

5. What does it mean to be teachable? If a man looks at his life, what are the signs that he's teachable or unteachable? How does a man become more teachable?

Chapter 6: Good Out of Bad

1. God brought good out of bad for the Washburn family. What good choices did the Washburns themselves have to make in that process?

2. Where do you see Proverbs 16:9 at work in Elimelech's story?

3. J. I. Packer said, "Though all human acts are free in the sense of being self-determined, none are free from God's control according to his eternal purpose and foreordination." How would you say that in your own words?

4. The author said God will bring good out of whatever is going on in your life. How does knowing that help you? Or how does it not help enough?

5. Edith Schaeffer said, "So the threads need to ask The Designer, The Weaver, The Artist, time after time to be used in the pattern where He would have them to be. It is not automatic." Is this asking just a matter of a quick prayer every morning? What else might it involve?

6. The author said of Romans 8:28, "We just hold up His promise and live off it. Instead of dwelling on our past and our failures, we look to Jesus—we fix our eyes on Him—and His promise to bring good out of tragic circumstances that resulted when we went our own way." What could living off God's promise lead you to do in your life?

Chapter 7: Hard Stretch of Highway

1. The author said, "Going through life on earth is like walking through an airport, pulling your black suitcase on wheels. Your real destination isn't some gate at a crowded airport; that's just the launch point." How should this perspective on earthly life affect the way we live day-to-day? Does it mean that this life and this earth don't matter?

2. Read Hebrews 11:1–6. In your own words, what is faith? What does living by faith involve, in practical terms?

3. Boaz was a kinsman-redeemer, or *goel*. In what ways is Christ our *goel*? How does He keep saving us?

4. Does it help you to know that waves of hardship are normal, that God uses them, and that they won't last forever? If so, how? If not, why not?

5. Read Psalm 107:23–30. When have you been in a storm like that? How should a person respond in the midst of such a storm?

6. Read Jeremiah 29:11. Jeremiah said this to people who would be in exile for many decades before the great and surprising outcome God had in store. If you knew it might take decades for God to bring something glorious out of your life, but you also knew the glorious outcome was guaranteed, how would that affect the way you live now? Would it be discouraging or encouraging? Why?

Chapter 8: Boaz Rides In

1. Boaz the farmer and Jesus the carpenter were faithful, reliable, and dependable. What do faithfulness, reliability, and dependability look like in your life? How does a man grow in these qualities if he didn't learn them from his father?

2. Os Guinness wrote, "We are not primarily called to do something or go somewhere; *we are called to Someone*. We are not called first to special work but to God. The key to answering the call is to be devoted to no one and to nothing above God himself." What motivates you to be devoted to no one and nothing above God? What can get in the way of that devotion?

3. If a man wants to trust the Lord when he's under brutal pressure from circumstances, what help does he need to keep doing that?

4. Randy Stinson and Dan Dumas offered these nine traits of a godly leader:

> Vision: *This is where we are going.*
> Direction: *This is how we get there.*
> Instruction: *Let me show you how.*
> Imitation: *Watch me.*
> Inspiration: *Isn't this great?*
> Affirmation: *You're doing great.*
> Evaluation: *How are we doing?*
> Correction: *Let's make a change.*
> Protection and Provision: *I'll take care of you.*

What does each of these mean? What does each trait look like in a family setting?

5. Sinclair Ferguson said, "That is why we can be quietly confident—not because we know exactly what God is doing in this unpredictable world, but because we know that what is unpredictable to us is already predicted by him." What encourages you to trust God in your current situation? What are the contrary voices that you need to tune out?

6. Psalm 50:15 (NASB) says, "Call upon Me in the day of trouble; and I shall rescue you, and you will honor Me." When has God rescued you in the past? How can you honor Him for that? About what situation do you need to call upon the Lord now?

Chapter 9: The Missing Piece

1. What attitude toward children do Psalms 127 and 128 convey? How does this attitude compare to the way men in your life view children?

2. What appropriate first steps did Boaz take toward Ruth? Why do some men become paralyzed or passive toward women? What can help them become able to move toward women with relaxed confidence?

3. How had Ruth been unsafe in the past? How was she unsafe when Boaz met her? How does her situation compare to what young women face today?

4. How did Boaz protect Ruth? How did he provide for her? How might a single man today appropriately protect a woman? How might he appropriately provide for her?

5. How does a good married man today relate to women other than his wife?

6. The Lord is good and does good (Ps. 119:68). When He gets a hold on a man's life, He turns that man into someone who can be trusted. What are the various ways you can be a trustworthy man?

Chapter 10: Man in Motion

1. Boaz was in an awkward situation when he woke up and found Ruth lying there. What are some awkward situations a man might find himself in today?

2. The author said, "It always comes down to the character of the man. Not his reputation, but his *character*. Some men work very hard on reputation and image. They want to look trustworthy. Ironically, these are the very ones who end up showing a deficiency in character." What is character? How is it different from reputation? Why is it more important than reputation?

3. Kent Weber told his future wife, "I know lots of men who strive very hard to be the real thing, who know God intimately and answer to something far greater than themselves. They are men who are humble, who respect women, devote themselves in marriage and families. They are men whose

genuine, disciplined lives model God's goodness in a myriad of ways." What does it take for a man to be the real thing? If he hasn't been the real thing in the past, how can he get there?

4. In what ways did Boaz refuse to take shortcuts? What are some shortcuts that men are tempted to take today?

5. Some men today are afraid of commitment. Why is that? What's good about commitment?

6. What are the top two or three things you admire about Boaz? How would you like to be more like him? What help do you need?

NOTES

Chapter 1: Boaz Man

1. Joel R. Beeke, *Jehovah Shepherding His Sheep* (Sioux City, IA: Netherlands Reformed Book and Publishing Committee, 1982), 18.

2. Owen Strachan, "Men, Temptation, and the Gospel," The Gospel Coalition, accessed August 6, 2012, http://thegospelcoalition.org/blogs/tgc/2011/06/02/ men-temptation-and-the-gospel.

3. Robert D. McFadden, "Jackie Cooper, Film and Television Actor, Dies at 88," *The New York Times*, May 4, 2011, www.nytimes.com/2011/05/05/movies/jackie-cooper-film-and-television-actor-is-dead-at-88.html.

4. Matthew Henry, *Commentary on the Whole Bible* (Grand Rapids, MI: Zondervan, 1960), 275.

5. Jeremiah Burroughs, *The Rare Jewel of Christian Contentment* (Carlisle, PA: The Banner of Truth Trust, 1648, 2005), 111–12.

6. Katie Burgess, "How many heart chambers does a worm have?," Wiki Answers, accessed August 6, 2012, http://wiki.answers.com/Q/ How_many_heart_chambers_does_a_worm_have.

7. Burroughs, *Rare Jewel*, 113.

8. Sinclair B. Ferguson, *Faithful God: An Exposition of the Book of Ruth* (Bryntirion, Wales: Bryntirion, 2005), 14.

9. Troy Meeder, *Average Joe: God's Extraordinary Calling to Ordinary Men* (Colorado Springs, CO: Multnomah, 2011), 2.

10. Arthur E. Cundall and Leon Morris, *Judges and Ruth: An Introduction and Commentary* (Downers Grove, IL: InterVarsity, 1968), 269.

11. John Flavel, *Triumphing over Sinful Fear*, ed. J. Stephen Yuille (Grand Rapids, MI: Reformation Heritage, 1682, 2011), 23.

Chapter 2: White Bread Gone Bad

1. Kip Fry, "America's Banker: The Many Chapters of A. P. Giannini," *The Journal of Financial Advertising & Marketing*, Financial Marketers' Alliance, accessed August 6, 2012, www.financialmarketer.com/node/71?destination=features%2Fartic les_insights%3Fpage%3D59.
2. Jim Collins, *How the Mighty Fall: And Why Some Companies Never Give In* (New York: HarperCollins, 2009), 6–7. Additional note of clarification from Collins: "In 1998, NationsBank acquired Bank of America and took the name; the Bank of America described here is a different company than NationsBank."
3. Fry, "America's Banker."
4. Rebecca Bertolini and Larry Richards, *The Smart Guide to the Bible Series: Joshua, Judges & Ruth* (Nashville, TN: Thomas Nelson, 2008), 123.
5. Dan Simon, "The gambling man who co-founded Apple and left for $800," CNN, accessed August 7, 2012, www.cnn.com/2010/TECH/web/06/24/apple.forgotten. founder/index.html?hpt=C2. See also en.wikipedia.org/wiki/Ronald_Wayne.
6. Thomas Watson, *The Godly Man's Picture* (Carlisle, PA: The Banner of Truth Trust, 1992), 12, 14.
7. Peter Marshall, *John Doe, Disciple: Sermons for the Young in Spirit*, as quoted in "Classic & Contemporary Excerpts," *Christianity Today*, accessed August 7, 2012, www. christianitytoday.com/ct/1998/august10/8t9072.html.

Chapter 3: Area 51

1. Annie Jacobsen, *Area 51: An Uncensored History of America's Top Secret Military Base* (New York: Little, Brown, and Company, 2011), back cover.
2. Jacobsen, *Area 51*, xi.
3. Matthew Henry, *Commentary on the Whole Bible* (Grand Rapids, MI: Zondervan, 1960), 275.
4. W. Gary Phillips, *Holman Old Testament Commentary: Judges, Ruth*, ed. Max Anders (Nashville, TN: Broadman & Holman, 2004), 302.
5. Iain M. Duguid, *Esther & Ruth: Reformed Expository Commentary* (Phillipsburg, NJ: P & R, 2005), 132.

6. Paul Tripp, "Depression and the Ministry, Part 1: The Setup," The Gospel Coalition, accessed August 7, 2012, http://thegospelcoalition.org/blogs/tgc/2011/07/11/depression-and-the-ministry-part-1-the-setup/.

Chapter 4: Rock or Sand

1. Eric Greitens, "The SEAL Sensibility," *The Wall Street Journal*, accessed August 9, 2012, http://online.wsj.com/article/SB10001424052748703992704576307021339210488.html?KEYWORDS=the+seal+sensibility.

2. Jonathan Aitken, *John Newton: From Disgrace to Amazing Grace* (Wheaton, IL: Crossway, 2007), 190.

3. Sinclair Ferguson, *Faithful God: An Exposition of the Book of Ruth* (Bryntirion, Wales: Bryntirion, 2005), 29–30.

4. John Newton, *The Voice of the Heart* (Lafayette, IN: Sovereign Grace, 2001), 209.

Chapter 5: Keep Calm and Carry On

1. Iain Murray, *David Martyn Lloyd-Jones: The Fight of Faith 1939–1981* (Carlisle, PA: The Banner of Truth Trust, 1990), 10–12.

2. Murray, *David Martyn Lloyd-Jones*, 11.

3. Murray, *David Martyn Lloyd-Jones*, 11.

4. Murray, *David Martyn Lloyd-Jones*, 11.

5. John Newton, "Disappointment—What Is Necessary—God's Patience," Puritan Sermons, accessed August 9, 2012, www.puritansermons.com/newton/Newt_j1.htm.

6. Charles H. Spurgeon, *Morning and Evening: A New Edition Based on the Holy Bible, English Standard Version* (Wheaton, IL: Crossway, 2003), February 14.

Chapter 6: Good out of Bad

1. Kerck Kelsey, *Remarkable Americans: The Washburn Family* (Gardiner, ME: Tilbury, 2008), 17.

2. Kelsey, *Remarkable Americans*, 229.

3. John Flavel, *The Mystery of Providence* (Carlisle, PA: The Banner of Truth Trust, 1662), 40.

4. Sinclair Ferguson, *Faithful God: An Exposition of the Book of Ruth* (Bryntirion, Wales: Bryntirion, 2005), 29.

5. Thomas Boston, "Of the Providence of God by Thomas Boston," Grace Online Library, accessed August 20, 2012, www.graceonlinelibrary.org/doctrine-theology/providence-of-god/of-the-providence-of-god-by-thomas-boston/.

6. Edith Schaeffer, *The Tapestry: The Life and Times of Francis and Edith Schaeffer* (Waco, TX: Word, 1981), 13–14.

7. Jonathan Edwards, *A History of the Work of Redemption* (Binghamton, NY: Vail-Ballou, 1989), 520.

8. Jeff Scruggs and Cheryl Scruggs, "Resources: I Do Again," accessed October 30, 2012, www.hopeformarriages.com/resources/.

Chapter 7: Hard Stretch of Highway

1. Brad Lendon, "Skeleton in bank chimney is of man missing since 1984, police say," CNN, accessed August 24, 2012, www.cnn.com/2011/CRIME/07/27/louisiana.bank.skeleton/.

2. Nancy Keates, "One Home, Three Locations: An author's nearly identical houses reflect his desire for absolute consistency," *Wall Street Journal*, accessed August 27, 2012, http://online.wsj.com/article/SB10001424052702303661904576453962563250044.html?mod=WSJ_hps_sections_realestate#project%3DSLIDESH.

3. Rebecca Bertolini and Larry Richards, *Joshua, Judges & Ruth*, The Smart Guide to the Bible Series (Nashville, TN: Thomas Nelson, 2008), 312.

4. Bruce Wilkinson and Kenneth Boa, *Talk Thru the Bible: A Quick Guide to Help You Get More Out of the Bible* (Nashville, TN: Thomas Nelson, 1983), 67.

5. R. Kent Hughes, *Ephesians: The Mystery of the Body of Christ* (Wheaton, IL: Crossway, 1990), 241.

6. John Flavel, *The Mystery of Providence* (Carlisle, PA: The Banner of Truth Trust, 1678), 127.

7. Matthew P. Mayo, *Cowboys, Mountain Men & Grizzly Bears* (Guilford, CT: TwoDot, 2009), 68.

8. Mayo, *Cowboys*, 72.

9. C. H. Spurgeon, *Lectures to My Students* (Grand Rapids, MI: Zondervan, 1954), 160.

Chapter 8: Boaz Rides In

1. Frederick William Farrar, *The Life of Lives: Further Studies in the Life of Christ* (Toronto, Canada: W. Briggs, 1900), 62–65.

2. Os Guinness, *The Call* (Nashville, TN: Word, 1998), 43. Emphasis mine.

3. Sinclair B. Ferguson, *Faithful God: An Exposition of the Book of Ruth* (Bryntirion, Wales: Bryntirion, 2005), 56–57.

4. Peter Marshall and David Manuel, *The Light and the Glory* (Grand Rapids, MI: Baker, 1977), 132–33.

Chapter 9: The Missing Piece

1. Rebecca Bertolini and Larry Richards, *Joshua, Judges & Ruth*, The Smart Guide to the Bible Series (Nashville, TN: Thomas Nelson, 2008), 318.

2. Arthur E. Cundall and Leon Morris, *Judges and Ruth: An Introduction and Commentary* (Downers Grove, IL: InterVarsity, 1968), 269.

3. Bruce Wilkinson and Kenneth Boa, *Talk Thru the Bible: A Quick Guide to Help You Get More Out of the Bible* (Nashville, TN: Thomas Nelson, 1983), 69.

4. John Phillips, *Exploring People of the Old Testament*, vol. 2 (Grand Rapids, MI: Kregel, 2006), 87–88.

Chapter 10: Man in Motion

1. Carolyn Weber, *Surprised by Oxford: A Memoir* (Nashville, TN: Thomas Nelson, 2011), 212.
2. Sinclair B. Ferguson, *Faithful God: An Exposition of the Book of Ruth* (Bryntirion, Wales: Bryntirion, 2005), 92–94.
3. Ferguson, *Faithful God*, 94.

Steve Farrar podcasts, videos, resources, and speaking info can be found at www.stevefarrar.com.

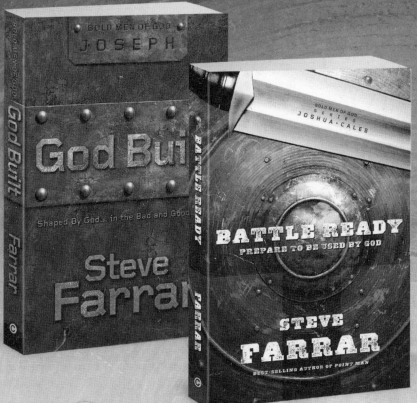

DISCOVER GOD'S REMEDY FOR FEAR

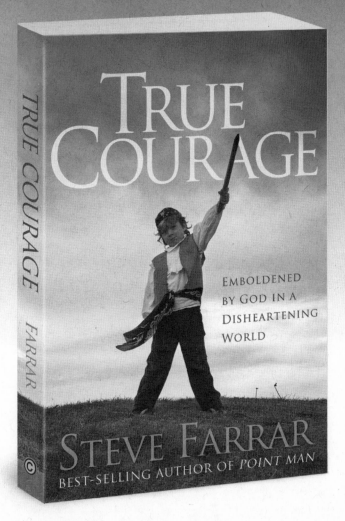

Everyone can recall as a young child having the courage to head out the door—whether it was to your first day of school, your first game in Little League, or your piano lesson. Then life takes over and you lose your bravado, giving in to the fears of the world around you.

In *True Courage,* readers will discover a God who provides incredible courage to us in the midst of uncertainty, even through treacherous, evil days, and the courage to face lions in their den—or an unexpected job loss, the diagnosis of a sick child, or the return of a debilitating cancer.